The Purple Pulpit

the
Purple Pulpit

Richard L. Keach

Judson Press, Valley Forge

THE PURPLE PULPIT

Copyright © 1971
Judson Press, Valley Forge, Pa. 19481

Bible quotations used in this volume are in accordance with the
Revised Standard Version of the Bible, copyright 1946 and 1952 by
the Division of Christian Education of the National Council of the
Churches of Christ in the United States of America, and are used
by permission.

International Standard Book No. 0-8170-0530-7
Library of Congress Catalog Card No. 70-147848

Printed in the U.S.A.

Contents

Preface

The title of this book, *The Purple Pulpit,* describes the process of conflict and change through which the people of Central Baptist Church in Wayne, Pennsylvania, are going.

For the past ten years, the pulpit, communion table, and lectern in the sanctuary have been gleaming white. One day an artist asked, "Why not antique purple?" He showed me a white clam shell which blended into a beautiful light purple around the edges. A purple pulpit, he felt, would be a symbol for the way a vital church must live its corporate life in the future. This color, which falls midway between red and blue in hue, is the color of conflict and change.

In biblical times purple raiment was worn by kings and nobles. As "King of the Jews" Jesus was derisively robed in purple. But although he wore a purple robe, he carried the cross. A people who would be servants of Jesus Christ will find the purple of conflict and cross-bearing a meaningful color.

The contents of this book have been lived by our congregation over the past few years. The words describe what I feel God has been saying and doing through his people in the Wayne church. This is not to say that God limits his action to one place. God is acting through other people in other ways. I say simply, here is one way. Hopefully, God is continuing through the Spirit to say and do some things on behalf of his kingdom through his people everywhere.

The book describes, too, the pain, frustration, failure, and celebration our church has gone through as it has sought to become God's reconciling agent in the world. It is my hope that, in reading about this process, others will be encouraged to enter into change within the church. For it is my conviction that this is the only way the church can move from its present self-satisfied inertia to fulfill its servant role in the world.

This book is dedicated to the faithful, devoted, and visionary people who have been or are now a part of Central Baptist Church. I am particularly grateful to Mary Lou Landon who typed the first manuscript, to Lawrence Janssen who encouraged me in the project, to Janice Corbett who gave the story order, to Allen Hinand who helped make and live the story, to my wife who shared with me the tensions of conflict and change, and to all the members who are part of the process in which we are engaged.

St. Davids, Pennsylvania
January, 1971

1. The Church Confronts Its Mission

On April 21, 1968, two hundred members of the Central Baptist Church, of Wayne, Pennsylvania, crowded into the fellowship hall for an unusual Sunday morning meeting. Emotions were running high. There was a tenseness that could almost be touched in the room.

As pastor of the church, I called the meeting to order and introduced the moderator who stated the question before the group: Should the church property be mortgaged in the amount of $100,000, with the money being used to serve the most pressing needs of the urban crisis?

I had been challenged when the idea was first discussed at a meeting in our home, following the assassination of Martin Luther King, Jr. It was proposed by the chairman of the board of deacons. A friend had called him a few days before and said, "Wouldn't it be a wonderful thing if the churches in the Philadelphia area called a moratorium on church building for a year and used the money in the urban crisis?" The group meeting in our home decided to propose a church mortgage for the same purpose. The figure of $100,000 was arrived at because it seemed large enough to be significant and not beyond our ability to repay.

Not everyone in the initial group was in complete agreement with the proposal. In fact, some members were violently opposed. In the business meeting at the church one person asked, "How many of us would mortgage our homes for the cause of human rights?" Another member shouted out, "Can I speak to that?"

He went on: "They ask us to mortgage our church property. It's easy to be generous with the property of others. We are being asked to commit this congregation to a financial burden of repaying $100,000 with $9,000 annual carrying charges for twenty years. This responsibility will continue long after most of us are gone. How many of the sponsors of this will be here ten years, or even five years from now? Why should we impose today's social needs on the future? I do not believe I have the moral right to saddle this church with a debt that others must pay."

A young woman rose to state her feelings. "I would like to say that I think it is unfortunate that it took a murder to get the church to take significant action. What we are talking about mortgaging is not really the church. The church of Christ, after all, does not consist of buildings and property. The actual church might even become stronger if the property were lost in an effort to redeem and reconcile members of our society."

Another person asked how the leaders of the church viewed such drastic action. One by one, each of the twelve members of the board of deacons stated his or her position. One said, "My wife and I were in South America during the hectic events following the slaying of Martin Luther King, Jr. We were glad to get home to discover what was going on. However, the first letter we opened in our stack of mail was the announcement of the proposal to mortgage our church property for the urban crisis. You can imagine what a shock this was to one who has been trained to be an accountant and controller, and for this reason is on the conservative side."

He went on, "To say that I have agonized over this matter is an understatement. But I am in favor of the mortgage for these reasons: First, because of my experience in working with the Main Line Community Association in trying to improve housing in our area, I've learned a lot in these last few months about the problems, the frustrations, and the needs. I've come to realize how difficult it is to get people and organizations, particularly churches, to become actively concerned and involved. I've become convinced that something dramatic and significant has got to happen in a hurry if anything worthwhile is to be accomplished. The motion we are voting on today could set a fire in this area that might have results far beyond our church — that would bring harmony, peace, and equality among our peoples."

As the debate continued, suggestions were made to return the resolution to different boards for further study and later action. Members wanted to know how the money would be repaid, what kind of projects it would be spent for, and why there seemed to be such an urgent need to act now. Countless individuals spoke for and against the plan. Sides were taken.

Finally, the time came for the 11:15 A.M. service of worship, and the issue was not settled. A motion was made that worship be canceled for the day, and the discussion went on. At 1:30 P.M., after four hours of struggle, the vote was taken on the original proposal, and the establishment of a Martin Luther King, Jr., Memorial Fund came into existence by a two-thirds vote.

THE ROAD TO CHANGE

Any minister would have rejoiced to hear in that meeting the eloquent and forceful testimonies of what the gospel of Jesus Christ means when people get down to the issue of putting money where the talk is. But our church did not reach that point of relating to the community's needs without struggle. It had been a rough, conflict-ridden road to change.

Central Baptist was founded in 1896 in the living room of Charles Walton, with the congregation numbering six families. These pioneering folk organized the church and built a building, which we still use, in the center of Wayne, an upper-class suburb on Philadelphia's Main Line. During the depression of the 1890's, the church survived by selling some land to a bank. About twenty years ago the Methodists and Baptists in Wayne even considered merging because their two congregations were so weak. However, they did not do so, and each church has continued its own ministry.

The people of Central Baptist have a heritage of caring. Many years ago a mission was begun in a Negro area of the town. Members of the church have had an active ministry in the Baptist Home (a retirement center in Philadelphia) and also in the Baptist Orphanage (now the Baptist Children's House). Individuals in the church have always been strong in giving to missions both money and personal service. The women of the church have ministered at the Valley Forge General Hospital, at Red Cross centers, at state mental hospitals, and at other similar centers. These acts of caring were significant. But they were also "safe." Our church, like so many others, was applying first aid to social needs, but not immersing itself in a depth struggle to bring about social change.

Many of the members of Central Baptist work in Philadelphia. Of the two hundred resident families, thirty-four people, many of whom are ordained clergymen, work for the American Baptist Convention at Valley Forge in the denominational headquarters. It would appear that this large number of clergymen have been the catalyst for change in the church. But one of the laymen says, "We have become involved in mission in spite of thirty clergymen."

The families who work for the denominational staff have been sympathetic to what the leaders of Central have been doing. They have taught classes and served on boards. They have participated in planning. They have contributed freely in the financial support of their church.

However, I am convinced that the church community would have moved in the way we have without the denominational people. We would not have moved so rapidly. The key to change in a church is the conviction of the ministerial staff. The rapidity of change depends on how much threat they can handle and how sensitive they are in reading the feelings of their fellow members. Movement is always going forward and pulling back.

A church that wishes to engage itself in total ministry to the world will need a group of lay people who are free enough to allow change to happen. There was a group (maybe twenty-five families) of men, women, and young people ready to move out. We began to build with these visionary disciples during the past seven years.

HOW CHANGE COMES

In 1957 I came to Central Baptist with a theology and mode of ministry which seminary had prepared me to perform and which fit the pattern of this church. This pattern included the idea that the way to change society is to change individuals. In three previous churches I had built a ministry on visiting the parish, preaching biblical sermons, teaching youth and adults in the church school, organizing small groups, and administering a program which was largely centered in the church building.

About seven years ago, I became convinced that the church would die unless it got outside the building and began to lose its life in servant ministry to the world, not only on an individual basis, but as a corporate people in the community. I became converted out of the church and to the world. This process came about gradually.

I had been reading Bonhoeffer's *Letters and Papers from Prison,* which opened a new concept about what it means to be Christ's man in the world. *Where in the World?,* the paperback by Colin Williams, confronted me with the mission of the church and how to structure ministries of the church beyond the building. An article by Jitsuo Morikawa in the book *Leaven,* edited by Paul Madsen, gave me a theological push to consider the purpose of God for the world, and the mission of the church in the world. Harvey Cox's *God's Revolution and Man's Responsibility* helped me to see the gospel of Jesus Christ in relation to the servant ministry moving outward.

A speech delivered at the American Baptist Convention in Atlantic City by Gordon Cosby, pastor of the Church of the Saviour in Washington, was a further challenge. He told the story of that church serving the world around Washington through committed servant living.

Articles, books, conversations, speeches all began to open a new thrust for my ministry. Two other experiences provided the motive for action.

A week of conferences at Princeton Seminary in 1966 with Professor Richard Schaull on the theme "The Gospel of Freedom in a Technological Age" put the picture into focus. We considered the implications of the collapse of old structures, life oriented toward the future, new symbols for a new humanity, new forms of worship and liturgy in the secular world. Ten days at the Institute for Advanced Pastoral Studies at Bloomfield Hills, Michigan, in January, 1967, opened me as nothing else had done.

Through the last seven years I have been on a new pilgrimage. My thoughts have been revolving around the issue: "What does God want of the church and of me in the new age? What is the mission of Central Baptist Church in Wayne, in Philadelphia, and in the world?"

The whole church has been invited to join in the pilgrimage and the struggle. As a result, we have begun to develop an adult education program geared to understanding the world so that we can minister in it. My preaching has taken a different direction. It is an attempt to interpret what God has done and what God is doing through his people in the world. The church organizations have begun to look outward instead of occupying themselves with housekeeping duties. The church boards have become involved in planning for mission and action.

Together, we have begun "putting our money — and our manpower — where the talk is." We have begun to move into the world as Christ's servants, living out the real mission of the church in our own community.

2. How Does Action Begin?

Convinced that the church must lose its life in order to find it, that the church must stop talking and begin living the servant life, groups of people in Central Baptist became motivated to act.

NONCONTROVERSIAL PROJECTS

The first action was simple and noncontroversial. A need existed in our community for an integrated nursery school. Two Negro communities on the edge of Wayne had no nursery school facilities. The white community had filled all existing nursery schools. Our education building was unused during the week.

The Minister of Education, Allen Hinand, organized the school. He found the teachers, set up the schedule and the tuition fees, advertised for children in the local papers, determined the salary for teachers, got scholarship money for needy children, opened the school, and then organized a committee to supervise under the general direction of the board of education at the church. Now, five years later, the nursery school is accredited, has six teachers, sixty pupils, and a waiting list. The school is self-sustaining, has purchased much of the equipment which we use on Sundays, and serves as a training center for girls from a nearby junior college who are learning to be nursery school teachers.

Another noncontroversial project was the placement of Cuban refugee families. The first family lived in the home of some church members who were away for the summer. Another member produced in his investment company a job for the Cuban father. He is still with the firm. Four other Cuban families have been sponsored by members of our church since the initial family became a part of our lives.

Still another type of noncontroversial corporate action was the sponsoring of students through I.C.Y.E. (International Christian Youth Exchange). This ministry was started at the suggestion of the American Baptist Home Mission Society. The board of education put $500 in the budget to sponsor a foreign student for one year. Students live in a church member's home, are given board and room and often clothing and expense money by the family. The $500 goes to I.C.Y.E. to pay for transportation and the expense of running the program.

In the eight or nine years we have participated, students have come among us from Germany, Greenland, Japan, Brazil, Nigeria, the Congo, and France. In the last four years young people have gone from our church to Brazil, Germany, Holland, and Sweden.

None of these actions, which were supported by the entire congregation, caused any conflict. There was a stated and felt need. People were organized to meet that need. Money was budgeted to complete the program. All of these projects are still going on.

CONTROVERSY DEVELOPS

In November, 1965, the following letter came to the church from the Wayne American Legion commander:

Dear Reverend:

As Deputy Commander of the 8th District, it is hoped at this time you and your officials deny those who speak out against the United States Government involvement in Vietnam privileges in using your facilities.

This group is very controversial and only ill feeling could come from such a meeting.

Let us now and forever stand behind our government.

Sincerely,

The deputy commander was referring to the Women's League for Peace and Freedom, which had requested the use of our fellowship hall for two public forums on the war in Vietnam. At that time the war issue was not being widely discussed, and no group along the Main Line would allow the W.L.P.F. to use its building. Since we were accustomed to letting community groups use our facilities, we had offered our hall for the forums.

The first forum was mild and instructive. Professors and citizens attempted to speak to the reasons for our involvement in Vietnam, and were both critical and supportive of the governmental position. The question period was lively.

The second forum came about a month later on a Sunday evening. By this time the American Legion commander had written the above letter, and the local newspaper editor had urged the church to call off the forum. In the face of rising opposition, our board of deacons met and carefully prepared the following response to the Legion commander:

The Central Baptist Church has always made its facilities available to outside groups for purposes of interest and importance to the wider community. We therefore granted permission to the Women's

International League for Peace and Freedom to use our Fellowship Hall for public forums on Vietnam.

In light of the continued publicity of these forums, your letter was referred to the board of deacons. This group concluded that two fundamental issues are involved: the freedom and duty of all persons to speak their opinions and the necessity for Christians to be involved in community affairs. Since this second forum is planned to include a panel discussion regarding the United States State Department's "White Paper on Vietnam" with learned speakers and audience participation, both these fundamentals will be fulfilled. The statement of the board of deacons does not represent any official position of our church, nor does it imply any endorsement by the church.

In discussion with our ministers, they have stated that as American Baptists we have a long tradition of maintaining the separation of church and state. This means for them that the church's role is not a role of rubber stamping our national policies, but is one of providing the opportunity for the expression of controversial views, still allowing the freedom of individual decision. They believe the Christian gospel to be a gospel that frees people from the fear of controversy, and a gospel that proclaims peace and unity between all men.

American citizens have enjoyed the right of free assembly. Therefore, we will continue to allow the use of our facilities in service to the community in keeping with American principles of freedom of speech and assembly.

Sincerely yours,

E. Duane Sayles
Chairman, Board of Deacons

This statement was published in both local newspapers. The ministers of Wayne met and put together a position statement on the role of the Christian in the war. The statement was read in every church on the day of the second forum.

About four o'clock in the afternoon on November 7, 1965, the police phoned to say they had received a call warning that a bomb had been placed in Central Baptist Church. The building was checked and no bomb was found. When the meeting began, thirty members of the American Legion stood at attention in the rear of the hall in dress uniform. The room was packed.

I opened the meeting by reading the deacons' statement. Trouble immediately started when one speaker chose not to salute the flag. Speakers were shouted down by calls of: "You dirty Communist!" "Traitor!" "Red!" A group of students outside chanted slogans and held signs through the windows which read, "Drop the bomb!" After about an hour of increasing confusion, five policemen came in and told everyone to go home.

Members of the congregation stood around at 10 P.M. that Sunday evening, literally shocked and troubled. The forum had involved us in a controversy we had not anticipated or sought. The issue had been one of free speech and freedom of assembly. But some segments of the community assumed the whole church was critical of the United States' position on Vietnam.

The deputy commander of the American Legion again expressed his opinion. In his letter he had called the meeting "the most un-American and ill-advised forum I ever attended. . . . As for your church, it left a black mark within. When my church [Catholic] adheres to such meetings then I will drop from their rolls as a member. . . . Not much can be said for your stupid deacons."

MEMBERS DISAFFECT

A few days later, after the newspaper had reported the stormy meeting, one of our members wrote:

I have been very much upset about what has been going on in our church. It seems a shame to desecrate the House of God by permitting controversies which "belong to Caesar" to take place on holy ground. I am ashamed of you.

He did not know that I was as upset as he was. Ten families withdrew membership from the church and a dozen others refused to make pledges that month in our Every Member Canvass. But then a new family joined — as a direct result of the forums — whose pledge equaled the dozen families who refused to give that year.

The forums raised a lot of hostility among all the members. They also raised hostility in the two ministers. They raised the issue which was expressed in the above letter. Do the people of God become involved in the world of Caesar? Is there a neat division between the things which belong to God and the things which do not?

In my own reading of the New Testament, I had been convinced that the things which belonged to Caesar also belonged to God. There was no division between sacred and secular. The whole world, including Vietnam, is in God's hands. Further, I believed that if no one else in the community dared to deal with "controversies," it was the responsibility of the church to become involved. This seemed to me to be the message of the cross and the meaning of incarnational theology.

A LEARNING EXPERIENCE

In the television documentary "A Time for Burning," the congregation in Omaha, Nebraska, could not deal with the controversy about exchanging families with a black church on a visitation basis. The issue became so divisive that the minister was asked to leave. That church's first big struggle ended in divorce.

In the days following the Vietnam forums, members of our church learned how to fight with each other and stay together. We learned what community can mean — and what it can cost.

We have faced many issues since then which have raised strong feelings. Two or three things have held our congregation together. One was a series of adult education programs which attempted to educate our congregation for change. Another was the adoption of a long-range planning process. A third was an examination of the roles which worship and preaching play in the life of a church.

3. Education for Change

When the Vietnam forum produced so much conflict in our congregation, the ministers invited a group of adults who were the most troubled to meet on Sunday mornings and discuss the role and mission of our church. We tried to deal with feelings. It became apparent immediately that we were a church full of people with different theological assumptions and different ideas as to how the life of discipleship should be lived. As one member put it, "A lot of people became Christians and joined the church to go to heaven some day. Now you have changed the rules and asked them to take up a cross and get involved in the world." He was right. The assumption of some members was that the church is a haven of refuge from an evil and terrifying world.

We soon realized that we needed a whole new set of theological assumptions. We also needed to know what kind of world we were living in so that we could move in it with knowledge and insight.

A NEW APPROACH

So it was that a new approach to adult education was begun in the fall of 1966. The board of education structured and offered six classes to adults. The classes met on Sunday mornings from 9:30 to 11:00 A.M. They continued for nine weeks. Four series were offered during the year. The first group included the following classes:

The Ins and Outs of Adolescents. This seminar looked at the needs and problems of the adolescent. It was an attempt to have adults understand the coming generation. The course was taught by a local doctor who had worked with youth for a long time.

Introduction to the Gospel. This was an introductory course to the New Testament. It was taught by a seminary-trained person who was living in the area.

New Members' Class. This class is required for all those who wish to join our church by profession of faith or letter transfer. The ministers teach the course. It is offered twice each year.

Uniform Lesson Series. This traditional adult class offered a series of lessons on the Bible. The first quarter was a study of the prophets. The class was led by two laymen in the church.

The Possibilities of Peace. A study of pacifism, appeasement, nonviolence, peaceniks, and nuclear pacifism was conducted by a woman active in the Women's International League for Peace and Freedom.

Black Power and the Church. Whites and blacks met to confront each other on the issue of power in the community. This class brought black leaders from the city of Philadelphia to our community for dialogue. It was coordinated by a member of the church with outside leadership coming in each week.

The classes were organized to educate our congregation to the role of the church in today's world. But they went far beyond the discussion level of most adult classes. Many led members into direct involvement in our community.

BLACK POWER AND THE CHURCH

The course on "Black Power and the Church" was based on Silberman's book, *Crisis in Black and White*. When the study concluded, the group was so interested in the issues raised that they decided to meet on Wednesday evenings and bring to their meetings people from Philadelphia who were working in the field of housing. The question was raised whether a suburban church could become involved in rehabilitating houses in a ghetto area.

About this time a local television station produced a program called *1747 Randolph Street*. The program revealed life in a city ghetto area called Ludlow, east of Temple University in Philadelphia. The documentary showed streets full of abandoned cars. Homes were empty, dilapidated, or boarded up. Ludlow was a forgotten area in city planning. In the program, Marvin Lewis, president of the Ludlow Community Association, made a fervent plea for help for some discouraged people.

The class persuaded the church to spend $1000, which was in the budget for city work, on research during the summer. A sociology student was hired by the church to live in Ludlow during the summer and work with the people of the area. He talked with people, walked the streets, met leaders, guided groups of our members through the area, and brought leaders from Ludlow to our church for dialogue.

At the end of the summer he wrote his recommendations. His opinion was that the most urgent need was for decent housing. Through his contacts with people in the Ludlow Community Association, we began to talk about housing needs. Some of our lay people began to spend many hours in the Ludlow area, meeting and talking with people. Finally a nonprofit housing corporation was formed. Five members from our church, five members from Ludlow, and one leader in the area became the official board of the Ludlow Housing Improvement Corporation. The group decided to rehabilitate empty houses. Funds were obtained from a denominational group. Central Baptist loaned $3000 as seed money for the project. A three-story row house was purchased. A local architect and builder were secured. It was planned that the building could be renovated into three apartments, financed by the Federal Housing Administration.

The first crisis occurred when a side wall of the house collapsed. The second crisis came when we found that the house would cost $38,000 to complete and an FHA loan could not be obtained to exceed $30,000. The house was finally finished with three beautiful apartments and sold to the Philadelphia Housing Authority for $32,000. The Ludlow Housing Improvement Corporation was almost bankrupt on its first venture. Starts were already being made on two other houses. These were stopped.

Again criticism was raised. Why was the church rehabilitating houses in the ghetto? What about the gospel of personal salvation? How is the gospel being preached in the Ludlow Housing Improvement Corporation? The action drove us to reflection and research.

Two of our men who spent the most time with the Ludlow program are insurance executives. After they had been meeting with people in Ludlow for over a year, one man asked them, "Why are you here? You can't sell us any insurance."

I am not sure what they said in answer to the question. However, I know that an authentic word of the Good News about Jesus Christ can be spoken when someone asks, "Why are you here?" It may be that ghetto dwellers who have heard so much talk about salvation and a better life in heaven will not be moved to listen to a word about Jesus Christ until they see that caring word lived out in concrete action, such as our members on the L.H.I.C. board delivered.

We were in Ludlow because we cared about persons and their lives. The gospel of Jesus Christ is to feed the hungry, to clothe the naked, and to help provide houses for people to live in. Jesus said, "Inasmuch as you did it unto the least of these, you did it unto me." The theology we attempted to preach was lived out in action. It was an incarnational gospel of "go into all the world and lose your life for others." If others saw the message in flesh, then our evangelism was authentic. The Word could be spoken when we were asked, "Why are you here?"

The Ludlow work continues. Two years ago a thrift shop was opened to sell clothing and furnishings which our church and other churches provide. The project began when a member of our church saw an article in the *Philadelphia Inquirer* about a woman who tried to sell her blood to get money for clothing for her family. Her blood had an iron deficiency and she was refused. The woman in our church asked, "Why don't we provide clothing so that the women in Ludlow could run a shop?"

One Sunday she passed out a folder outlining her plan. She asked for volunteers who would bring one piece of clean clothing a month. She had a good response from our church and soon had enlisted several other churches in the project. Our church serves as a collection center and each month volunteers from the church transport the goods to the thrift shop.

After the thrift shop had been in operation for about a year, a report was given to the church which included the following items:

—The shop has contributed $1000 to the Ludlow Community Association.

—It has provided part-time employment for five community women.

—It has given emergency financial assistance to a number of families.

—It has provided clothing without cost to seventy-five children, enabling them to attend school.

—It has provided carfare to community boys to attend sporting events in the city.

—It has subsidized a community evening at the "Playhouse in the Park."

—It has sponsored a community picnic for children.

—It has provided food baskets for families at Christmas.

When we voted the Martin Luther King, Jr., Memorial Fund, two allocations were made for Ludlow programs. The sum of $5000 was given for a summer program to hire fourteen young people to work on voter registration, in tot lots, and in community cleanup. The people of the area raised another $6000. A further gift has been allocated to the Ludlow Community Association to begin a day-care center for children, so that mothers on welfare can work and have a place to leave their children.

The Ludlow Housing Improvement Corporation continues to function. The group is currently seeking to enlist a local builder to do rehabilitation of homes with the Ludlow group serving as helpers. Since the initial involvement of the Sunday morning class in housing needs of the city, other groups have begun to work in the Ludlow area. Education is education for change. The purpose of our adult education program is to open adults to the world so they may respond to it in mission.

THE INS AND OUTS OF ADOLESCENTS

Another early class in the new adult curriculum was on youth culture. A local doctor gave his time for nine weeks, leading a group of adults to an understanding of the youth world of music, art, language, and religion.

This class met in the basement community room of the Wayne Federal Trust Bank building. On the first Sunday I stumbled into a dark room with music blaring and lighted by one candle up front. On another Sunday I was summoned by a policeman who said he had a warrant for the arrest of the class because they were disturbing the peace. On that Sunday the class was hearing music the young listen to. The policeman had the entire class on tenterhooks until they discovered the teacher had arranged the whole thing to show adults what it is like to get hounded and picked up by the police!

From this class and other similar programs, a community youth center opened in Wayne in October, 1969. "The Inner Sanctum" is the result of five years of effort on the part of many citizens of our community and members of Central Baptist working together.

For two years Central had organized and operated a teen center on Friday evenings for junior high youth. The program met in our fellowship hall and was supervised by fifteen students from nearby Eastern Baptist College. While working with this group, about thirty alienated youth were discovered. People from the youth culture class, two of the young adults in particular, decided to meet with these thirty kids on Thursday afternoons. They had a difficult time. The kids were tough to handle. Communication with them was nonexistent. The workers learned how hard it was to break through to the world of these kids. They tried to live out a caring theology of concern with limited success. In these months of work, windows were broken, as well as furniture and relationships. They never did learn how to get the gospel across to this group, except in a caring, love-in-action way.

Their work brought the problem into focus. We began to reflect on our action. The Wayne ministers were enlisted. Each church pledged $100 for a summer program. A seminary student was hired for $1000. He lived in our church house and ran with that bunch of alienated kids all summer. His strategy was to be present and to attempt to spin off some of the kids to a different way of life. At the end of the summer, when Jerry returned to seminary, the kids had a party for him. He received a sweater from two of the gang members with a note attached which said, "You are the first one who has ever really cared."

That was a stormy summer, too. The kids climbed up the drainpipes all over the church building, pulled them down, and threw the small stones from the education building roof over the church yard. They broke windows about every week, which upset the church members. It upset me, too, until a counselor mentioned one day that the most Christian thing we could do was to provide a place where they could break a window.

One of the members of the board of trustees resigned

that summer. At a special meeting called to deal with the crisis of breaking in, he said, "I've got more to do than attend special meetings about these kids. Lock up the church on Sunday afternoon and unlock it the next Sunday morning, and we won't have any problems."

A neighbor called one evening to say, "When are you going to get the police to clear that gang off your church property?" That fall this group of thirty had adopted the steps of our church house as their security spot. They were there before school at 7:45 A.M. and back at 3:15 P.M. when school closed. They stayed until dinner time and often returned until dark or later, which they still continue to do. On this particular evening the neighbor was walking her dog and some of the kids were necking on the porch. This bothered her and she wanted me to drive them off our property. I explained what we were trying to do and invited her support to meet with them. She begged off.

We learned that many adults, even church members, did not want anything to do with this bunch of "unsaved kids." Their gospel was, "When these kids get washed, get their language cleaned up, get their habits improved — when they learn how to act as we do — then let them come around." The call of Jesus to leave the ninety-nine and go search for the one did not seem to apply to this situation right on our church steps.

Determined to move the problem to a solution, I called a meeting of community leaders. We looked at the teen situation in our area from every angle. Out of a series of meetings a group was formed called WAYNE INC. (Wayne Area Youth Need Encouragement), composed of Protestants and Roman Catholics.

WAYNE INC. formed a nonprofit corporation which raised $10,000 from service club donations by sponsoring the community charity ball, by helping in the community Independence Day celebration, and from church and individual contributions.

For two years the group searched for a place to begin a teen center. During that time a youth organization called "The Inner Sanctum" was born, and it promoted monthly programs for senior high youth. In the spring of 1969 a building was made available for rent from the township commissioners. It was renovated and opened in October, 1969. The center has dancing facilities, a snack room, a lounge, a game room with pool tables, and other possibilities. It is open every day after school for junior high age youth, and particularly for the alienated group who hang around our church. It is open on Friday and Saturday evenings for senior highs. Long-range plans include working with the schools and the guidance people of the area to reach all youth, especially those who feel cut off from the rest of society.

This teen center has taken five years of planning, acting, studying, making mistakes, trying, plodding, prodding, until finally the community responded to a need. The role of Central Baptist was to keep the problem before the eyes of community leaders until it could not be ignored. Again, an adult class that was being educated about teen culture and was becoming aware of the strategy of prodding was instrumental in launching a ministry of action to youth.

These two ministries have been described in order to show how a group of adults, open to what is going on in the world and bringing a theological assumption about the meaning of being present in the world, can move in a constructive way. The educational philosophy behind the adult class curriculum is to make adults aware of the world of human need. With a theology of "go ye into all the world," and "except you lose your life you cannot find it," and "taking the form of a servant," education will lead to action and change in the social structures of society.

Since we began our broader adult education program, many adults in the congregation have learned about, or been exposed to, the world of black power, Vietnam, the city, the Kerner Report, Roman Catholic theology and practice, welfare rights, the problem of abortion, civil disobedience, Jewish thought, and many other subjects, as well as the Bible and Christian faith. (A listing of the subjects offered in the adult education program in recent years will be found in Appendix 3.) The purpose of adult education, as we see it, is to examine the world in the light of our theological assumptions, and to measure the effectiveness of our theology by the reality of the world.

STUDY FOR NEW MEMBERS

The early class led by the ministers for people disturbed over the Vietnam forums convinced us that we needed a membership class for all persons joining our church, so they would know what kind of theological and sociological assumptions are held by the ministers, and what the ministers and other members of the church are trying to be and do.

We had always had courses for new members. Many of them were held on Sunday evenings or week-nights. With a suburban church it was difficult getting regular attendance. Over the years we experimented with different kinds of curriculum. For several years we used *The Ministry of the Laity* by Francis Ayers.

When the Sunday morning schedule of study from 9:30 to 11:00 A.M. was initiated, we devised an adult new members' class that would do what we wanted. The class format changes each time it is presented, but it generally includes a look at contemporary culture, theological assumptions, history of the church and of Central Baptist, and a study of baptism and Communion. The class is held twice each year, usually in the fall and spring. Adults who wish to join the church by baptism or transfer of church letter are required to attend. Many persons who are already members voluntarily attend the classes in order to gain new insights and relationships.

After experimenting for at least ten years with baptismal classes for youth, lay people in our church worked out a six-week curriculum. We started the class on Saturday mornings by inviting every young person in the church from the seventh grade on up who was not baptized or who had not yet made a decision to accept the Lordship of Jesus Christ and to join the community in servant living. The movie called *The Parable,* originally shown at the New York World's Fair, was used the first week to set the overall concept we intended to share: that the follower of Jesus Christ is a servant willing to risk for others. In all our sessions we used small-group sharing and discussions to explore the subject. (A fuller description of the curriculum for these sessions will be found in Appendix 3.)

When the sessions were concluded we made individual half-hour appointments with each young person. In these encounters we discussed the class itself, the ideas that developed, the meaning of Christian discipleship, and we asked each person about his or her decision. There was no pressure to get the whole class baptized. However, we baptized over twenty-five one Sunday morning.

This chapter has not attempted to describe what is being done in the children's and youth educational divisions. They have followed a similar approach of exposure to mission, but have generally relied on more structured denominational curriculum resources, rather than adopting the elective principle of the adult division. The message of involvement appears to have gotten across in these age groups too. A ninth-grade class was asked, "What did you like (or dislike) about your church school class this year?" One boy said, "I like the class to talk about some of the problems of the world — and to find out what we can *do* about them."

Education for change has helped us to become involved in our congregation and community. It has prepared us to assume our mission in the world.

4. Strategy and Planning

At about the time we were struggling to define our purpose and mission as a church, a group called Metropolitan Associates of Philadelphia, an action-research organization, began to develop a program for organizational planning. Richard Broholm, a member of the board of deacons who was employed by this group and has since written a book called *Strategic Planning for Church Organizations*, suggested that we use their strategy to plan for mission.

The church cabinet appointed a nine-person committee to deal with the purpose and mission of Central Baptist Church. For a year this group met every other week at 7:30 A.M. in a local restaurant to fashion such a statement.

The strategic planning process calls for a group to first list its theological and sociological assumptions. A statement of purpose and objectives based on these assumptions is then developed. From these, strategies and tactics for carrying out the objective are formulated. (The complete statement of purpose, assumptions, and objectives will be found in Appendix 2.)

We have been developing programs to accomplish our theological and sociological assumptions. A permanent committee on planning is developing the planning document as a plan for mission. In preparing for the

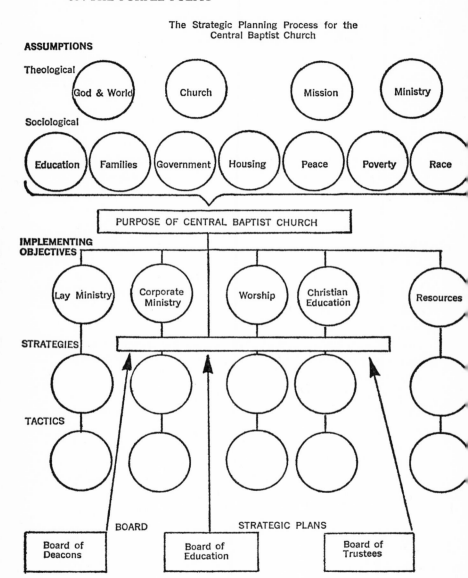

The Strategic Planning Process for the
Central Baptist Church

ASSUMPTIONS

Theological

God & World   Church   Mission   Ministry

Sociological

Education   Families   Government   Housing   Peace   Poverty   Race

PURPOSE OF CENTRAL BAPTIST CHURCH

IMPLEMENTING OBJECTIVES

Lay Ministry   Corporate Ministry   Worship   Christian Education   Resources

STRATEGIES

TACTICS

BOARD   STRATEGIC PLANS

Board of Deacons   Board of Education   Board of Trustees

stewardship program of raising funds for the year's work, we arranged the budget according to the priorities outlined in the strategic planning process. In the future we hope to spend our money according to our theological and sociological assumptions. (See Appendix 5 for an illustration of the way in which the planning process was applied in preparing the 1970 budget.)

At first, the board of deacons assumed responsibility for dealing with the objectives of worship and life, lay ministry, and corporate ministry. The board of education developed ways of implementing the objectives for education and worked with the deacons on lay ministry and corporate ministry. The board of trustees developed tactics on the use of property and buildings for mission.

Then, during the fall of 1970, a bylaws revision committee suggested that the church reorganize its major board structure in terms of the strategic-planning objectives. Instead of the boards of deacons, Christian education, and trustees, the committee proposed new bylaws which provided for boards of lay ministry, corporate ministry, worship and life, Christian education, and resources. The new bylaws were presented to the congregation and approved so that the church could be reorganized along the lines of the strategic objectives.

As an example of how we have worked on the long-range strategic-planning process, let us look at the area of worship and life and see how the board of deacons (before reorganization) developed strategies and tactics in relationship to the objective for this area.

OBJECTIVE:

Through thoughtful study and experimentation we will strive to integrate more effectively the issues and concerns for our daily work with the way we celebrate on Sunday morning, in order that our work may truly be an extension and expression of our worship, and our worship the offering up of our work.

STRATEGIES:

To accomplish this objective, we must on a personal, local community, national, and international level identify those issues and concerns which are faced by our people in their home, school, work, or other environment, and structure our worship activities to meet effectively the challenges in these areas by:

1. Encouraging the interpretation of the social and other changes taking place in our work and in our communities in the light of the purposes and needs of our worship.

2. Determining the worship needs of our membership through person-to-person contacts, taped comments, group meetings, etc.

3. Developing the awareness that worship needs to be and can be extended outside the church building.

4. Exploring and evaluating new concepts and techniques of worship as possible avenues for broadening the scope and deepening the experience of our overall worship program.

TACTICS:

1. In order to relate our worship services more closely to our lives and work, we must explore the use of small groups as worship cells. While these worship cells might be made up of the present study groups, the formation of new special emphasis groups should be investigated. The interest expressed in our early service Communion breakfast indicates that perhaps Communion could be included in some small-group activity to make this ordinance more meaningful.

2. There is some feeling that our educational program is not properly stressing the place of worship in our lives. Our church school should conduct a study course for our young people in the meaning and purpose of worship.

3. The expressions of the senior highs in their taped comments in the Sunday morning service are of deep concern. In order to obtain feedback on the kind of worship which would appeal to this group, we will commission them to structure a worship service as they would like to see it carried forth.

4. Other useful and meaningful forms of worship will be investigated, such as, drama, music, dance, dialogue, etc.

5. As a means of obtaining better overall coordination and direction in our worship activities, the entire board of deacons should undertake a study of worship.

TASK ASSIGNMENT:

1. Small-group worship
   To deepen the worship activities in our present small study groups, the following procedure under the direction of chairman of the worship committee is suggested:

   a. Meet with one representative from each of two of our present study groups to obtain their ideas on small-group worship. Immediate future hosts might be appropriate persons.

   b. Initiate (if they agree) trial for two meetings of adding more in the way of worship than at present.

   c. Suggest slanting refreshment period as an informal Communion.

   d. Survey members of these two trial groups for reactions after first and after second meetings.

   e. Report to board after second meeting with recommendations for expansion or formation of other types of small groups.

   (To expand on small groups program, it is suggested that the worship committee chairman, with advice from the pastors, explore the formation of additional study groups. These might be composed of such special emphasis groups as new members, college students, etc. Report to board in June meetings before taking action in any new direction.)

2. Church school study of worship

   It is suggested that the chairman of the board of deacons contact the chairman of the board of Christian education to explore this general field of worship education in the church school. While the basic responsibility for such a study will be with the board of education, the board of deacons has a substantial interest in the program and should lend its support and assistance. Assuming that the board of education would be interested in pursuing such a program, the chairman of the board of deacons should appoint a member of the board to be a one man education committee to work directly with a designated member of the board of education to develop a program. This committee would be charged with designing and introducing the study course, considering such things as:

a. Curriculum;

b. Integration into Wednesday and Sunday programs;

c. Age group or groups to be included;

d. Length of study;

e. Teaching staff;

f. Relationship to new members and other study activities.

3. Senior high worship project

A member of the worship committee should work with the senior high group to help them develop their ideas on worship service structure.

4. Use of new forms of worship

5. Deacons' study of worship

These two tactics (4 and 5) seem to closely related that they might best be carried out under the same project, as follows:

a. The worship committee could schedule a series of three special meetings of the board as worship workshops (June, September, and November).

b. The worship committee will be responsible for workshop agenda, study materials, background information, assignments, etc.

c. The latest materials on worship from ABC offices and from other denominations should be explored as source material.

d. Formal report to the board, suitable for presentation in our annual report, should be made by January, covering the conclusions and recommendations growing out of the worship study.

MAIN LINE COMMUNITY ASSOCIATION

Another example of how action for change resulted from a study of strategy was the formation of the Main Line Community Association. The board of deacons, working on the objective of corporate ministry, met for one winter with the deacons from a nearby black church, First Baptist in Mount Pleasant, to consider what the mission of these two churches in Wayne was to be. They concluded that a most pressing human need was for low-cost homes which minority families could afford. Our two churches decided to enlist the other churches of the area in an association to deal with this problem.

Two of our deacons worked with the black and white communities and began to organize churches and synagogues. It took two years of hard work to enlist twenty Protestant, Roman Catholic, and Jewish churches and groups into an association dedicated to making life just and human for all our citizens. The Association meets monthly and concerns itself with fair housing problems, construction of homes, repairs on homes, and other issues concerning the poor, the powerless, and the overlooked minorities.

After the group had been meeting for a year, the Association formed the Main Line Housing Improvement Corporation, and, with $15,000 obtained from the Martin Luther King, Jr., Memorial Fund from Central Baptist, purchased six acres of land on which twelve low-cost homes for low-income families will be built.

The group has also met with the American Baptist Service Corporation and is looking for land on which to build large-scale, low-cost housing for low-income families, a need which is urgent in order to relieve the housing shortage in Philadelphia, and to enable black families to break out of the white noose that surrounds the city.

Other projects also have been a direct result of our strategic planning process. The new emphasis on meaningful worship is one. Many more projects — both within and outside the church — will develop as the individual task groups work through their objectives to strategies and tactics.

The strategic-planning process has provided a framework for our mission which prods us to meet new human needs and, at the same time, insures that our action grows out of our basic common assumptions about the church and the world.

5. Preaching for Mission

As Central Baptist began to face conflict and change, we agonized over the role of preaching in mission. Many parishioners hoped that the sermons would not change. They came to the worship services for comfort and security from a hostile world. But the challenges which faced the church called for a new pattern of preaching.

THE SPIRIT AND PREACHING

Preaching is an interpretation of what God has done among his people and what they are doing in the world to bring in an order of justice and love. If the Spirit has not come to a congregation, there is not much to interpret. Yet the church is rare indeed where a stranger can drop in on Sunday morning and feel caught up in an exciting group of Christians among whom the Spirit appears to be working. This lack must be one reason, maybe a central one, why so little comes from the thousands of sermons that are preached every week in American churches.

The question of how the Holy Spirit invades a congregation is a central one. Surely it begins in the pulpit with the minister convinced that this is God's world, that God as Spirit is ready to break in, and that there is need for the clergy and the laity to be open to the

Spirit. The whole business of theological study, Bible study, prayer groups, sensitivity groups, cell groups, and all the rest, could be the means by which the Spirit of God will break open a congregation.

In reality, the churches which are the most ready to move into dynamic action in the world are churches with a history of attention to the Holy Spirit and the cultivation of the inner life of the soul. Nothing will happen in a church until it is a body of people who believe the Spirit has come and will come to weld them into a community of people who, to use Rollo May's description, "can love outward."

PREACHING AS LOVE IN ACTION

Loving outward is doing the works of God. Love in action is what the parable of the good Samaritan was about. Love in action is Matthew 25 — food for the hungry, drink for the thirsty, welcome for the stranger, clothing for the naked, visits to the prisoners. Love in action is "emptying oneself" — taking the form of a servant, and being willing to get nailed for the mission of Jesus (Philippians 2).

When love in action is occurring in a church, then preaching becomes an interpretation of what this means. Sermons are never monological, irrelevant, harmless homilies, for they interpret the action of God through this people.

During the time Barry Goldwater was running for president of the United States, I preached a sermon entitled, "Was Jesus a Conservative?" I used the passage from Matthew on "You cannot put new wine into old wineskins." The sermon was an attempt to state a position on the role of Jesus and the church in the

whole national scene at that time. It was also a statement on how God moves in every age to speak to his
people through new forms, new ideas, and new ways.

That Sunday an executive and his wife stormed out
past me saying, "We are never coming back through
this door again." This response was more real than,
"I enjoyed your sermon."

However, the aim of preaching is not to drive people
out of the church, but to drive them into the real world
to be engaged in the mission of Jesus Christ. The aim
of preaching is to enable the Spirit to change lives, open
lives, and speak a Word which can be heard and put
into life.

ACTION PREACHING

I was trained in seminary to believe that preaching
could change the way a congregation moved. As an associate minister to a master biblical expository preacher,
I became convinced that expository preaching could
move a congregation. I didn't understand at that time
what mission was, beyond reaching persons for Jesus
Christ and bringing them into the church, all the while
loving them and providing structures where they could
feel loved and wanted. In that church situation we all
served each other by teaching, singing in the choir,
serving on church boards, living moral lives, and giving
to missions.

Since then, I have served in other places where I was
not sure that sermons had any role in actually changing
people's attitudes and their behavior patterns. In one
church I talked about love for several years while many
members of the congregation continued to harbor hos-
tilities. When I left, the same people hated the same

people. Perhaps the reason that preaching did not change attitudes and behavior was because the Spirit had not come, the church was not engaged in action, and, therefore, the sermons were impotent.

For five years at Central Baptist, my sermons were mainly expository. I would take a book from the Old Testament in the fall and do a series of sermons, always making an application to the common life we had together in the world.

Most of my sermons in those years had a personal application. Their purposes were to help the congregation think through an issue, feel better, leave with hope, meet a problem, sense the presence of God, be committed more completely to Christian discipleship, give more money for the church and missionaries, learn how to pray, feel forgiven, care about others, and be informed about Christian doctrine.

So it was in those years that one of our members commented: "Preaching is the worst means of communication we have. Why not do away with the sermons? We could gather for worship, break into small groups to discuss the theme of the day, and return for a concluding hymn and benediction."

About that time we became involved in the Vietnam forums, Ludlow, and the youth gang ministry. As a result of all that was happening to me, my preaching underwent a drastic shift. The sermons became more and more an interpretation of the action in which the congregation was involved.

One of the meetings of the board of deacons in 1965 was devoted to the subject: Is our pulpit really free? Can the minister preach what he feels impelled to preach? People were saying: "Quit talking about Viet-

nam, civil rights, Ludlow, mission in the city, poverty."
They also included in their list sex, death, and other
unpleasant subjects. When I made a little list of the
off-limit subjects, only motherhood, the nation, and
the sins of others were left for sermon exposition.

We discussed the freedom of the pulpit in a long
and agitated session of the deacon board. We agreed
that the pulpit should indeed be free. We also decided
that continued sensitivity to people's needs and fears,
plus a balanced diet of sermons, would probably be
wise.

It is difficult to stay off "hot issues." If biblical preaching is to interpret what God has done and what God
is doing in and through a congregation, then sermons
will hit close to controversy most of the time. My
theological assumption for preaching is that God is involved in all the world. None of the world is outside
his care. Further, he calls us to be reconciling agents
of healing in his world.

Surely there is a limit to what preaching can do in a
congregation. However, there are some things which
interpretive sermons can do. They can help make clear
what God is doing. They can reveal the signs of where
and what God is doing. They can describe how God is
acting. They can lay a biblical groundwork to see and
discern the action of God. They can show that the
world we face is not very different from the one which
Abraham or Paul faced. They can present the call to respond as faithful stewards, and show us that we are as
reluctant to get involved as Moses was to go to Egypt
or Jonah to Nineveh.

This type of preaching can be done in an exposition
of either the Old or the New Testament. One year

I spent three months on the Book of Joshua. I was amazed in studying the book to discover how many passages have modern implications which immediately excite the imagination.

Between Christmas and Easter that year I preached ten sermons from First Corinthians. Again, this was an attempt to interpret what God was doing among the members of Central Baptist.

THEOLOGY AND PREACHING

If preaching is an honest attempt on the part of the minister to interpret the action of God in the world, it must be based on an authentic experience with God. Out of this experience, the minister develops a relevant theology which is basic to his interpretation of God's action.

The theology which I have developed through the experience of conflict and change follows.

GOD AND THE WORLD

This is God's world. He created it and made man. He is working in the world — the entire world. There is no separation of sacred and secular. God is working for justice and love in the events of men in this world.

God came to Moses as I EXIST. Whatever the experience meant, Moses was called to go down to Egypt and to help get the slaves out. In the early books of the Old Testament God appears to be going before individuals and his people, calling, leading, pushing them to come out of whatever condition they are in and to be a people of freedom and justice.

As the Jews wandered in the wilderness, God appeared to them as a cloud by day and a pillar of fire

by night. I believe the writers of the narrative are saying that Yahweh, the Holy One of Israel, is the One
who exists and goes before us. God, then, is the One
who goes before us, leading us on to a land which lies
ahead. The land can be called the Promised Land, the
kingdom of God, or utopia. It is the "not-yet."

The role of the person who seeks to be faithful to
God is to discover for himself who God is and what
God is doing in his world.

When we had the Vietnam forums in our church, the
member of the church who wrote me the letter about
the shame of desecrating the church had grown up in
the church. His theological assumption was clear. The
church was "holy ground" and a sacred place. Discussion of the war in Vietnam was a secular issue and God
had no concern with it, except perhaps to see to it that
the forces of good beat back the Vietcong.

My primary assumption is that the entire world is
God's. God is concerned about war, civil rights, poverty, class, the missile race, and every other issue which
concerns justice and being human. Nothing, therefore, is off limits for the people of God to be involved
in.

MAN

Man is both good and demonic. The opening chapters of Genesis demonstrate that man was created to be
a steward over creation. God gave man power to name
the animals, dominate the earth, be fruitful and multi-
ply, and to create a place out of the desert where life
could be good and noble. Man and God, working together, were building a place which would be called
"the kingdom of God." The goal of human life is, in

the words of an old hymn, to "make the earth fair and all her people one."

From the beginning a problem developed in achieving this goal. Sin entered because God gave Adam and Eve free will to "do their own thing." Man's sin is twofold. Sometimes he is hung up on pride and sometimes on apathy. When God warned his two created beings to leave the tree alone, they discovered that the tree held powers to make them like God. They ate the apple.

The writer of the story is telling us that man's sin is pride. He does not want to be a steward over the garden. He wants to run it. He doesn't want to be a collaborator. He wants to be the boss. He wants to run the world and run people. He wants to play God.

The white man has been playing God with people of color for many centuries. He has made them his slaves. He has exploited them. The sin of the white man in America is what he has done to the American Indian and to the black man out of a sense of pride that he is better than they are.

The other sin of man in the early stories of Genesis reveals the sin of apathy and "passing the buck." Eve let the snake tell her what decision to make concerning the apple. Adam let his wife tell him what response to make and then blamed the action on her. The stories of Cain's refusing to assume responsibility for killing his brother, and the descendants of Cain refusing to be human, show us man begging off his role of steward and collaborator with God to make the earth fair and just.

The executive who went storming out the church door one Sunday saying, "We are never coming back through this door," never did. I talked with the family.

The wife said, "My husband works hard all week. He deals with Negroes in labor unions and gets in deep struggles with them at the company. When Sunday comes, he wants to find a haven of refuge from all that. You just give him more controversy and involvement and we don't like it."

Again, the theological assumption of these people, who had been in the church for thirty years, is clear. For them, being a Christian had nothing to do with being concerned and involved in God's black and labor world as a steward and collaborator. The secular world was something bad that one had to put up with in order to make a living. The church was that place of retreat where one could forget. They did not need to be reminded that man's sin from Adam was refusing to assume responsibility for the whole world. They surely did not need to hear about that in worship.

Yet, white people in the church are not alone in having difficulty with the sin of sloth. For three hundred years black people in America have heard from their churches the theological assumption that one day when you die God will make it all right for all the years of slavery. The sin of the black man in America has been the sin of apathy. The militants are largely outside the black church, preaching a theology which is very biblical: "Black is beautiful! Assume responsibility for the world God has given you! You don't have to be a victim of the white man's sin of thinking white is best. Tell him to take his foot off your neck, for you are a man and a person."

JESUS CHRIST

Every generation has shaped its own unique understanding of Jesus Christ. To the first Jewish Christians he was the Messiah spoken about by Isaiah. Some segments of the Reformation made him the stern Lord of the Last Judgment. In medieval art, Jesus was the fat-legged infant in the lap of the serene Madonna. In our time, Bonhoeffer called him "the man for others."

The Jesus who "turns on" this generation is the man who was nailed on a piece of wood for the life he believed in. This Jesus is a servant, a self-emptying person who spent his days with the poor, the lonely, the forgotten, the unloved, the hungry, the imprisoned.

For me, the crucial Christ events are the incarnation and the resurrection. The primary question is: How can the servant Jesus be incarnated in me? How can the life of servant love, a risking love willing to get nailed, be lived out in the body of a people called the church?

Incarnation theology is the only theology which carries authenticity in our world. When persons see justice and caring love lived out in parents, teachers, and in the corporate action of the church, they pay attention.

Resurrection theology is open-ended theology. The central issue is not so much whether and how Jesus was resurrected from the grave, but how can I become resurrected from old dogmas that no longer live, old ideas that deserve to die, old habits that are sterile? The issue is whether I can become an instrument of resurrection for those around me and for the church in which I live and move. Just as Jesus had to go into the grave and die in order to be resurrected, so an individual and a church will have to go through the grave in order to discover the meaning of resurrection.

Let's face it, the institutional church looks little like a resurrection place. It looks more like a coffin about to be lowered into the grave. Denominational programs and studies by church committees will not guarantee a resurrection. When the church or an individual becomes willing to get nailed for the cause of Jesus Christ in the world by taking risks, he will die little deaths and begin to act like a resurrected being.

In Central Baptist, we have seen persons go through death and resurrection and come out as fiery, dedicated followers of the Christ, willing to become involved in all of God's world. When the church faced the decision to borrow $100,000 and set up a Martin Luther King, Jr., Memorial Fund for the urban crisis in the Philadelphia area, lay people stood in a business meeting and made powerful statements of faith about their commitment to what God was trying to do through us. It was like the old-fashioned testimony meetings, only this time the testimonies were about the church's mission in the world, and not hung up on personal piety about getting one's own skin saved. More than anything else, the witness was about living out the servant life in God's world for others.

MISSION

I have always believed that Acts 1–4 is basic to an understanding of a theology of what the mission of the church is. After Jesus was nailed on the cross, the scattered disciples wandered about in confusion. One of them gathered the group together in a room, where they were told to wait. The Spirit came at Pentecost and welded them together into a community that moved into the world "with one accord." In his first sermon Peter began to interpret what was happening.

In Acts 3, the church moved into action and became a people of redeeming love. They were resurrected from discouragement. They became agents of reconciliation and resurrection. Again, Peter interpreted what God was doing through this new community. In Acts 4, their action brought persecution, which made the community stand together more firmly.

The point is clear. The gospel of love is not created by words. First the Spirit made them into a community. This empowered them to put love into action. Finally, words interpreted what was going on. Culbert Rutenber, in *The Reconciling Gospel,* describes the order of witness as "Be — Do — Say."

In the kind of world we live in, nobody is paying much attention to the endless flow of words which come out of the church, out of denominational headquarters, out of ecclesiastical gatherings, out of the thousands of pulpits in the land. They are looking for love in action.

When the church becomes an instrument of justice and risking love — doing acts of love for the poor, standing in the midst of racial strife, being with the lost and the lonely, marching against the threat of missile war, getting involved in welfare rights — then the words which come out of the church will ring authentically and clearly.

The church, then, exists to be a servant of Jesus Christ in the world. Its word is spoken best when people ask the question, "Why are you here?"

The year after we voted on the Martin Luther King, Jr., Memorial Fund, more members were received than in any year of the church's history. Many who joined said, "We read about the church in the paper. We like what the church is doing. We believe in what you stand for. We want to be related to a church like this."

When a church begins to live its theology, its witness is heard. The story of Jesus Christ, the man for others, the servant of God in the world, begins to carry some clout. The church exists for mission, for servant ministry, and only when it carries out this ministry is its message believed.

STRENGTHENING THE PREACHING MINISTRY

Preaching for mission demands a constant dialogue with the congregation. The minister is not the only person in the church who perceives God's action in the world. He needs the insights of others to supplement and inform his understanding. He also needs to know how his words have been received — what people have actually heard.

For two years a deacon has gathered six persons together after worship some Sundays to discuss such questions as: (1) What did the sermon say to you? (2) What do you think the preacher was trying to say? (3) What would you like to tell him about preaching? (4) What changes of attitude or behavior do you see coming out of the worship and sermon? (5) What difference do you think the message will make in your life?

This is done several weeks each year. The conversation is taped, and I listen to it later in the week. I have learned what people hear in relation to what I thought I said. Helpful suggestions and critical comments have improved both worship and preaching.

In the fall of 1969 an adult class met on Sunday mornings to study the book of First Samuel, from which I was preaching for three months. The group spent a half hour discussing what happened the past Sunday with the sermon. Another hour was spent discussing the passage on which I would write the sermon for the next Sunday. We considered the role of preaching, the function of a sermon, the communication barriers which exist between the preacher and the congregation, the authority of the Bible, as well as studying First Samuel in some depth. We also considered how the sermon contributed to what worship is all about.

My preaching has been strengthened by the conflict and change which our church has experienced. In turn, preaching has produced even more conflict and change. But this process has led to growth for our whole congregation.

6. Worship that Celebrates

As Central Baptist faced its mission in the world, many of us began to feel the need for more relevant worship. We have experimented with many new forms of worship in an attempt to find meaningful ways to celebrate our corporate existence and purpose. In July, 1969, a group of students from Temple University came to worship with us. They had talked to us in June about coming to share their concerns. I had informed the congregation the previous Sunday that they were coming.

The group said, "We want to do our own thing." In the service we moved through the hymns, prayers, and liturgy. As I started to preach, a voice thundered out of the baptistry, "Jeremiah! Where are you?" The voice continued to call.

A bearded figure in burlap came down the aisle and began to repeat Scripture from Jeremiah—Scripture about closed ears, unseeing eyes, and cold hearts. After a few passages other students came forward, also dressed in burlap, and proceeded to beat up poor Jeremiah, leaving him lying on the chancel steps.

Jeremiah struggled to his knees and addressed the congregation, "We have come here today as a disruptive force to share our concerns with you." Back down the aisle came the six other students. Each one chose a small section of the congregation and began to address the people in that section. They told about themselves and what was on their minds. During all this time other students in the choir loft were beating on bongo drums and the piano. The voices and music built to such a confusing climax that I expected to see people leave. No one did. Suddenly everything stopped. Another girl stepped down the aisle and began to address the congregation. She said, "I have grown up in the church. In recent years I have been disillusioned about the church's involvement in the world around it. I have not seen many churches risking anything to live the servant life. What is this church doing to be faithful to its purpose, its prophets, its Lord?" For the next thirty minutes the congregation tried to communicate with the eight students. When we closed the service, sixty people adjourned downstairs where dialogue went on for another hour and a half.

WORSHIP IN A SECULAR AGE

Five years ago a group from our church attended a conference at Green Lake, Wisconsin, on "Worship in a Secular Age." The questions raised by the conference were, "In a secular age, can worship become a means by which the transcendent breaks in? Is it possible for people who live in a world come of age to sense anything of God in a worship service of liturgy, hymns, prayers, choir music, and preaching?" Some of our high school students and young adults had been saying for a long time that what we were doing on Sunday morning at 11:00 o'clock said nothing to them.

During the last few years, there has been a lot of talk around our church about worship being "the celebration of what God has done in the world, and is doing through the life of this congregation." Members said, "We talk about worship as celebration, but there is little celebration in what we do at the times we say we worship." The conference at Green Lake did one thing for us. It raised the question of what we were trying to do when we gathered for corporate worship. Our deacon board has been helping the church deal with this issue for five years.

People over fifty years of age who have stayed with the church have no trouble with the question, "How do you worship in a secular age?" They see God as transcendent, as personal, as Spirit and Love. The gospel hymns, the long pastoral prayer, the choir selections, the liturgy, the sermon — they all help to create a "spiritual" atmosphere. These things "make them feel better," give them "something to take home," provide a connection to what they remember as a religious experience. For these people worship is a remembering.

One of my minister friends calls all this kind of worship "participating in a superstition." He claims that most of the 2,500 members in his church read Christianity as a "spiritual" experience. They participate in worship in order to feel good.

This kind of worship has little confrontation in it. The order of service uses music coming from other centuries and biblical and liturgical material focused on personal piety. The preaching may be up to date, but it usually centers on the person's relation to God and makes Christianity a religion for people committed to Christ, who apply the gospel in a personal way.

CAN WORSHIP COOL A GHETTO?

For me, this view of worship is seriously lacking.

Keith Watkins asks in his book *Liturgies in a Time When Cities Burn,* "Can such a pietistic liturgy cool the summer?" Detached liturgy can cool the suburbs and keep the church as the protector of the status quo. A so-called "spiritual" liturgy can preserve the values of those who have already "made theirs."

However, worship which gives the vice-president of a corporation a spiritual pat on the back will not cool the restless ghettoes or bring in an order of justice for the poor, the oppressed, and the victimized.

One church member said, "I've had a hard week and I want something to take home so that I can get through next week." Anyone can appreciate the need for direction and courage to live with a confusing schedule and a week packed with appointments which drain physical and emotional energy. In answer to this statement, I said, "I do give you something to take home — 'Except you lose your life you cannot find it.' Jesus told us that we would find joy, peace, and the courage to live as we got involved and immersed in life."

The theology that says the fruits of the Spirit can be packaged and delivered on Sunday mornings so that each member can take his portion home and feed on it all week is erroneous theology according to the way I read the New Testament. "Except you lose your life you cannot find it" cannot be packaged and delivered through a liturgy. This kind of cross-bearing gospel carries its own fruits and delivers these fruits in places often far from worship centers.

CELEBRATING WHAT GOD IS DOING

So the question arises again, "What is the place of worship in a gospel which asks for taking up one's own cross for Jesus Christ in the world?" If the theology of this gospel is correct, then worship is the celebration of what God has suffered on behalf of the world, and the occasion to learn where one can join God in his suffering in the present world. Worship becomes the means of attaining vision and insight into places of human need, getting courage to go from corporate worship to that place, and beginning to lose one's life.

After we had restructured our worship to say these things, one member began to express discomfort and to stay away. At a luncheon meeting he confessed that worship made him feel guilty about his not being involved in mission in the inner city. He did not like this feeling of guilt and decided to stay away from worship. He worked in a large corporation and had a position of influence. I tried to say, "Forget the city. God has placed you in a position of power. What do you think God wants from you in that place? How can you bear the sufferings of God in your company structure?" It was an attempt to help him see that to be a Christian meant for him to be asking the theological question of God's mission where he worked.

He has not come back to worship. However, I believe that worship did what it intended to do. My executive friend got the idea that worship has to do with one's action on behalf of God in the world. Since his whole experience with church had been around personal piety, he was not prepared to respond by losing his life in the life of the world. The call to "go" produced guilt and this was uncomfortable. He alleviated the guilt by staying away from the church.

When a church is losing its life in mission and servant living in God's world, then it has much to celebrate on

Sunday morning. Worship, in this light, becomes the celebration of what God is doing through these particular people in the world to make life decent and human.

On that morning of April 21, 1968, when our congregation struggled for four hours with the proposal that we mortgage the church and give the $100,000 away in programs for jobs, housing, and education, we voted at 11:00 o'clock to cancel the formal worship planned for the day and to go on with the proposal.

Most of the four hours were a time of celebration. Statements of affirmation were made, rededication of life was promised, the world was affirmed or rejected, faith in the future was professed or doubted. The liturgy was the life story of where we had been going as a church for the past years. The sermon was preached by many persons with moving eloquence. When at last we voted to go ahead, the whole morning could be described as a time of celebration for what God was doing in the world and what God would do through our action.

Perhaps the reason so little comes from the thousands of worship services held each Sunday morning in America is that the order of mission in Acts has been forgotten. The order of mission is "Be — Do — Say." When the Spirit produces a community which moves into the world in acts of love, then "Say" (worship) takes on eloquence and power.

WORSHIP TO CELEBRATE MISSION

Perceiving worship as celebration has led us to change many worship traditions including our order of service.

There are three sections in our service of worship: beginning, hearing the faith, and returning. These sections describe the purpose of worship. We praise God. We hear the faith stated and applied to life. We return to the world to live it out.

The preparatory statements set the theme for the day. These have included quotations from newspapers and magazines, poems, a brief statement about public servants, a historical vignette. Over a period of time the whole purpose and expectation of worship has been set forth in these preparatory statements. They are short and delivered from the floor level of the sanctuary.

Many of these preparatory statements and other worship materials will be found in Appendix 4.

Affirmations are usually from Scripture passages. They also contain contemporary applications. The affirmations are selected to deal with some development of the day. They affirm our historical theology.

Confession has come hard to our congregation. When we first began to use prayers of confession, centered not only on personal matters but on social issues, some people did not want to confess the sins listed in the liturgy, for they had not committed any of these sins.

Most people do find it rather jolting at the beginning of a service to say, "Our Father, we confess that we have not been consumed with compassion for the brokenness of human life in Philadelphia." "God, we confess to feelings of smugness and superiority because of our race, our church membership, our theology, our Main Line mailing address." "We confess our inability to feel the pain and despair of the poor person, of the black man hemmed in the ghetto, of the Vietnamese family ripped apart by death." "We confess that we have widened distances rather than built bridges. We have worshiped myths rather than de-masking them. We have avoided confrontations with the realities of the world."

I was bothered that we could feel so self-righteous, so lacking in the need of confession. I wrote a prayer of confession which began, "O God, we confess that we can sit here today in this quiet sanctuary and feel nothing to confess."

Sometimes the congregation is asked to read the prayer of confession in silence and if some do not wish to join in when it is read in unison, they may remain silent. Surely each man should have the opportunity to confess his own sins.

The words of the minister announce the pardon which God in Jesus Christ has already given to us. Pardon and forgiveness are also given by each member of the congregation to his neighbors, to those who sit beside him, and to those he will meet tomorrow in his world.

If a church is a community of those who have received the Holy Spirit, then there needs to be a time for the community to give forgiveness and receive forgiveness. Often on Communion Sundays during this giving of forgiveness we will pause to shake hands and greet those who sit near us.

For many years I have felt that readings from both Old and New Testaments were helpful in hearing the faith. Discussions in the worship group revealed that some people do not listen to the readings. A section called "The Bible in Life" is an attempt to speak a contemporary word on the theme of the biblical passage. There is opportunity for great variety of expression here. In our early service of worship where there is an attempt made to seek new forms of celebration, one Sunday I asked for people to relate incidents in their lives where the biblical passage for the day made a connection. Another time a young woman came down the aisle singing "How Can People Be So Heartless?" from the musical *Hair*.

The use of music in worship as celebration is important. We use the classics, folk ballads, trumpets, violins, guitars, and we have begun to gather a selection of hymn words written by members of the congregation. We are working on producing our own hymnbook with words and music which speak to our time.

Pieces of sculpture have been used instead of flowers on the retable. During the Advent season a four-foot sculpture of the Madonna and Child was loaned to the church by a local artist. Also, during one Advent season, children and adults spent three weeks making banners which were used to decorate the sanctuary. On one Easter morning the service opened with primary and junior children marching into the sanctuary with banners they had made on the Easter theme. These were hung up all over the church and provided color and message for the celebration of Easter.

On a Reformation Sunday a Jewish choir presented a service of Jewish music, our choir sang the Roman Catholic Requiem, and we concluded the service with Luther's hymn "Ein Feste Berg." This Sunday service was the result of a class meeting on Sunday morning concerning the subject of Jewish-Christian dialogue. Our youth have used drama and dance in celebrating God's action in our world.

This whole attempt to find new forms led us several

years ago to put into the service a time for sharing "concerns of the congregation." This period comes after the sermon and the pastoral prayer. During the concerns I come down to the floor level and share my own concerns. These may include a new baby born into the church community about whom I say something personal, the death of a member of the congregation for whom we have a brief memorial, the sick who are in the hospitals. There may be concerns about issues facing our community or the nation. Many of the concerns come from members of the congregation who are invited to share them with the community.

When we first started this time for "concerns of the congregation," no one spoke. However, after four years, it is a rare Sunday that one or two persons do not share a deep concern about the church family or the human family in the world outside and ask for support.

When we began to sponsor Cuban refugees, the committees, the houses, the jobs, all came in response to sharing the concern with the people.

When the antiballistic missile vote approached in the Senate, a member rose to say how important it was to state an opinion on this matter. He and another person would be at the doors to receive one dollar from those who desired to send a telegram to either or both Senators from Pennsylvania. Members could vote either yes or no. About thirty persons had their fellow members send telegrams in their names.

During the winter of 1969 an appeal was made on behalf of some families in Norristown, Pennsylvania, who did not have food or heat in their homes. By the next Sunday we had collected two station wagons full of food, and $200 to buy coal and oil. We continued to work with the helping agency until that particular crisis passed.

Fifty years ago when everyone knew what was going on in the town, friends could rally to meet a need. Today when our church congregation is spread out for miles, the time for sharing concerns serves to bring us together as a family who will share goods and time with those in need.

The offering of tithes comes at the conclusion of worship. After we have heard the faith, we respond with our money. The manner of our reponse is an indication of whether God has made us into a people who will act upon our professed faith.

A standing invitation for people to take the first step in affirming Jesus Christ through our church, in baptism or by transfer of church letter, is printed in the service bulletin each week. As these families come forward, they are introduced and wait at the front of the church to be greeted by many who come to meet them after the benediction. The benedictions are always said in unison.

A meditation appears on the back bulletin cover. It is selected from novels, plays, books, poems, and usually it casts insight on the theme of the day.

NEW FORM OF CELEBRATION

Besides the service described above which is held at 11:15 each Sunday, there is an early service from 8:45 to 9:30 each Sunday morning. The worship and life committee of the deacon board worked on experimental worship for two years in an attempt to produce forms and liturgies which speak to those attending this early service who have difficulty with older forms. The service is held in our fellowship hall. Chairs are arranged like this:

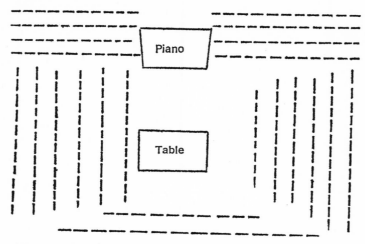

The service begins with singing around the piano. A special hymnal has been put together and mimeographed. We now have fifty modern hymns, many of them with words written by members of the church.

The words of preparation may be given by the worship leader from the middle of the square. Sometimes we begin by saying, "Worship is celebration of what God has done and is doing. What have you found to celebrate this week? What has God done in your life this week to cause you to affirm life?" People contribute whatever the Spirit leads them to offer. These words of celebration are gathered together by the leader into a statement of affirmation.

The prayers of confession are usually more open and bold than those used at the 11:15 worship. Silence is used frequently for private confession and forgiveness.

At this service we have experimented with guitars, recordings, background music, audio-visual material, dialogue sermons, and drama. We are constantly seeking new ways to celebrate what God has done in Jesus Christ and what God is doing among us.

Many Sundays there is time for dialogue after the sermon. The sermon will be ten or fifteen minutes long, with dialogue for another ten or fifteen minutes. These opportunities for a continued exploration of the sermon theme have proven to be moving times. Sometimes the discussion seeks to deal with feelings of anxiety, fears, hostility, or a different interpretation of the text than the one the preacher has presented. At other times, the dialogue moves the subject into unexplored areas. Sometimes practical suggestions are offered which can be acted upon.

CELEBRATION IN COMMUNION

On the first Sunday of each month Communion is observed in most Baptist churches. In an attempt to make Communion a time of celebration and community, the deacon board suggested a Communion breakfast at 8:30 A.M. on the first Sunday of each month. The deacons prepare the meal and have organized a group to set up tables and arrange details. We began this service with three tables of ten people each and the attendance has grown ever since. For example, on the first Sunday in December, 1969, there were twenty tables, all full.

For breakfast we have juice, which is also used for the cup, loaves of bread, cereal, milk, and coffee. The value of the service is the value of the old family night dinner which churches used to have. Children, youth, and babies come to the Communion breakfast. The nursery is open for the last part of the service and small children leave.

The service begins with singing hymns around the tables. Hymns like "Lord of the Dance," "Thank You," "Come, Thou Long-Expected Jesus," "In Christ There Is No East or West," and songs like, "They Will Know We Are Christians by Our Love." "People," and "To Dream the Impossible Dream," are often used. The opening prayers are followed by the sharing of the bread. The loaves on the tables are broken and passed around. The words for the bread conclude the first part of the service.

When we have eaten, the service continues with music, Scripture, and Communion reflection on the Scripture. The message is delivered from among the tables. During the concerns, new people are introduced and new members are received, in addition to the sharing that occurs each Sunday.

The cup comes at the conclusion of the offering. The closing litany serves as a statement of dedication.

The Communion breakfast, the sharing of concerns, the new forms of worship which we have developed are attempts to let worship become a means by which a group of Christian disciples can celebrate what God has done on behalf of man, and an attempt to become faithful servants of God in the world.

7. Freedom to Move

How does a church free itself to reach out in mission to its community? One of the first steps is to involve the minister. A congregation which has been doing house-keeping duties for years on behalf of its own members will never turn around and relate itself outwardly in servant living unless the minister is willing to enter the struggle.

THE MINISTER IS THE KEY

The minister in the Protestant church is the agent of change or the keeper of the status quo. He is determined either to lead a congregation to pick up the cross and follow Jesus, or to putter around in the safe ecclesiastical structures. If the minister does not want the congregation to be involved in the world in God's mission, the church will never be involved. Even if a group of people within the church gets restless for change, the minister can turn off the heat and blunt their energy for mission. No matter what kind of church government there is, the clergyman holds the key to keeping the congregation locked up or let loose.

The first step for any group of people in a church who want to move ahead into reconciling ministries which may be controversial is to enter into study and dialogue with the minister to see where he stands.

Likewise, if a minister wants the congregation to turn itself outward in servant living, his first step is to get with those people in the church who are like-minded. He can invite them to meet with him at his home, gather groups for breakfast or lunch, or get lay people to organize groups where he can be present.

At the same time, he will need outside emotional support for his own needs. He must find some like-minded person who can listen, encourage, and support him. This person may be a denominational worker, fellow minister, trusted layman, a counselor, or psychiatrist. He will need the friendship and guidance of this person over the years.

The reason some clergymen never get on with breaking a church loose is that the situation seems impossible, the people in control too entrenched and immovable. Furthermore, most ministers have not been trained in seminary to do this. They know how to be chaplain of an institution, but not how to organize a guerrilla force to start an infiltration.

A minister can get a group together. He can find a helper. Then he can start reading and thinking with the group. They can read Harvey Cox, Dietrich Bonhoeffer, Colin Williams, and others. They can ask over and over, "What do we exist to be and do?"

As the group gets organized, they can discover a situation of human need in the community which no one is meeting. This situation may or may not be controversial. They can plan a strategy of involvement and organize a task force to learn and act in the situation.

If controversy does develop, the group's strength and commitment will be tested. Nothing will let a minister know more quickly who can stand up under heat than to be caught in a sticky situation. When Central Baptist was pushed into dealing with what happened over the Vietnam situation, it became clear who would stand up for the right of free speech and free assembly, and who would run away.

PEOPLE WHO MOVE

There are many types of people in a church. Every congregation has a group who become members for social and religious reasons. They say, "Everyone should belong to a church. Our friends go there. It is good for business. You can't get married without a church. The Sunday school will give our children some Bible teaching. It makes me feel good to support the church. I can meet people that way. Our family has been in that church for three generations."

Some people want comfort and peace. They are harassed and need a haven of refuge. From childhood, heaven and eternal life have been a hope for them. Moral living, attendance at church, giving, singing in the choir, teaching church school — they all help to insure a life after this one. All this participation gives them comfort.

Adults who come from conservative families where smoking, drinking, movies, dancing, and golf on Sundays were sins have probably rejected all these taboos now, but have hangover guilt feelings. Belonging to and supporting a church helps to alleviate this guilt.

In every church are old liberals who have been freed from the dogmas of the virgin birth, the literal interpretation of the Bible, the physical resurrection of Jesus, and the second coming. They are emancipated from dogmas, but stay in the church for other reasons. What these people usually lack is a theology of God working in the world and through the church. Their Christianity is sometimes pietistic. They are good, moral people. However, they have no intention of picking up the cross and getting involved on behalf of the poor, the helpless, the powerless black. It is extremely difficult to enlist these Christians in "losing their lives for Jesus' sake." Such a response costs too much and is too threatening.

In every church are many dependent people. Freud attacked Christianity because it made people dependent and prevented them from growing up. Bonhoeffer said such people use God as a crutch. The Gospels and Paul's letters call Christians to "grow up in every way." This is a goal for a Christian or a congregation to achieve. If there are many dependent-type people in the congregation, it will be almost impossible to move that church to involvement in any significant way.

What is necessary to begin to move is a clergyman free enough to risk rejection and some people mature enough to see that Christ calls his disciples to risk and involvement in all the world.

LAY MINISTRY

Who knows what makes a church a mature community of servants? Whatever circumstances did combine through the years to produce a people with a high sense of responsible churchmanship, I was impressed the first time I met the people at Wayne. There is little internal quarreling over petty matters. A high sense of commitment to living out the gospel of Jesus Christ has been present. The nucleus of persons who can be counted on has been significant. It was on this dedication and willingness to serve that we were able to build.

Central Baptist is not a clergy-dominated church. The giving of time and life to the Ludlow ministries, to the Main Line Housing Improvement Corporation, to the teen-center work, to teaching, to cooking meals, and to everything else we have undertaken has come from lay people.

Bruce Copeland, one of our laymen who works in an insurance company, once said,

Whether we like it or not the future of our cities and our country is being shaped by the institutions where we work. Here are the centers of power and decision-making. So my understanding of lay ministry is that I should get my company to see its mission as a corporate citizen with responsibilities to help solve problems of our society and not just in maximizing profits.

I first developed a strategic plan. Next I approached the company's senior management group to discuss the social issues of our time, with specific suggestions as to how our company could significantly affect such change.

Multimillion dollar mortgage investments in housing for low and middle income families and a large increase in employment of minorities are two visible areas of our company's involvement within the last couple of years.

Here in this area of lay ministry our church should be helping laity so we can close the loop of total involvement from our homes, through our church, through our voluntary activities, and through our jobs.

Bruce had been thinking about his role as a Christian in his company for some time. Several years ago he joined a group of men in Metropolitan Associates of Philadelphia (MAP). These men meet regularly to see what can be done from within to reorient the city's power structure toward social change. MAP is an experimental "research-action" agency. It attempts to develop a style of lay ministry in the institutions and structures of the city.

Bruce sees himself as a lay associate, related to his job, MAP, the local church, and the other places of the city where he is personally involved.

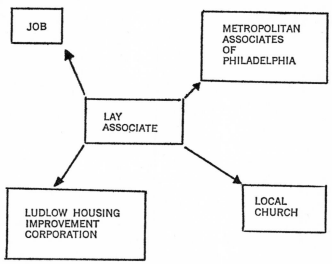

By seeing his job as the most important place where he can affect social change in the city, or to put it theologically, to help reshape God's world toward the New Creation, Bruce can see the local church as helping to prepare him for this task. This concept of lay ministry does not get hung up on expecting him to spend all his time and energy attending meetings and oiling the ecclesiastical machinery of Central Baptist. His primary area of Christian discipleship is at the insurance company.

Belonging to MAP helps him forge his tools to "think

theologically" about his job. He really feels that this enabling ministry is the function of the local church. This is a giant step from the view of the man who said, "Don't bring the world of Caesar into the church." When an executive or a laborer asks, "What does God want of this business, this school, this organization?" then he is asking the right question.

LAY MINISTRY AND THE CHURCH

We have reached the place in the church where we must now train lay people to know how to move in large corporations, in small businesses, and everywhere in the world as God's reconciling and changing agents. Those who know what it means to assume responsibility for the world move in this world with different assumptions than those who think the world is an oyster with a pearl in it and their role is to find some way to crack it open and get the pearl for themselves.

For years the church has emphasized personal piety for businessmen. Christianity has meant to be as honest as possible, maximize the profits, keep your personal life morally clean, get your soul in order for heaven, join the important church in town, and support foreign missions to convert the heathen.

In a discussion about being responsible stewards in God's world, I asked a lawyer, "How would you move to deal with the question, 'What does God want of our law firm?'" He thought awhile, then said, "But we can't begin the day with prayer!" It is not his fault that the only connection between law and theology he had been helped to make by Yale and the local church was to pray with his fellow lawyers as the day began, a practice which would embarrass them all.

Ralph Nader says the legal profession must be reformed if society is to be cured of its ailments. Instead of dealing with social ills, Nader claims the best lawyers spend their time defending Geritol, Rice Krispies, and the oil-import quota. A theology of lay ministry on the part of lawyers who belong to the church might radically change all this. Lawyers who see themselves as stewards of God and collaborators with God would probably be spending time on problems such as air and water pollution, racial justice, poverty, juvenile delinquency, and prison reform.

The role of the church in working with lawyers, for example, would be to get a group of lawyers together on an ecumenical basis and begin to reflect on what it means to be a lawyer and a servant of Jesus Christ in God's world. A task force of lawyers, bankers, teachers, salesmen, policemen, or any other group, reflecting biblically and theologically about their profession, is one way to move in order to bring about social change.

The church in America can begin to play a vital role by helping its laymen learn how to become change agents in the governmental, financial, and professional institutions where they spend their energy and time.

8. The Community in Conflict

A church which has begun to move toward change will need to develop a plan for dealing with conflict. A group may be formed to formulate theological assumptions for mission, then to study the community and work out sociological assumptions, and finally to develop objectives and tactics.

Education is important. Adults need to be exposed to and informed about the world we live in and how the gospel of Jesus Christ meets that world. Preaching and worship will help interpret to a congregation what God has done and is doing in the world through this people. Members of a congregation will have to discern and identify the action of God in the world before they can relate themselves to it.

FACING CONFLICT

Even while the initial study is going on, the minister and groups of people will encounter conflict and hostility. It will come from all directions. Those who joined the church for social reasons will complain that the church has forgotten its members and has gone off into social action for people out there whom they don't even know.

Those who want peace and a haven of refuge will attack the minister for not providing "spiritual nourishment." They will say, "You are not making me feel good with your sermons." The minister will have to listen to this criticism, for the gospel is both comforting the afflicted and afflicting the comfortable.

The conservatives will become angry. They will feel more guilt because they are not out there "where the action is" working for social change, or be angry because someone else is. Since they have been burdened with guilt feelings since childhood, they will be quick to feel guilty again, especially since they do not want to go beyond pietism to radical involvement in gut issues in God's world.

Social action will also make "old liberals" feel guilty. When they begin to feel guilt or anger over not being involved in struggling for social justice, they will gradually drift out of the church.

Dependent people will become very threatened when a church gets embroiled in controversial issues. Talking about black power, militants, civil disobedience, lazy welfare people, peace marchers, or dissent will raise their anxiety level to the place where they will find it difficult to stay in the situation. Their inclination will be to run away to a safer place.

When a minister and a group of people begin to open a congregation to the bleeding world outside the church, there will be loosed a torrent of anger and rejection. Can they deal with it?

The minister's first inclination will be to run away. He may think of leaving the church for another place. He may consider leaving the parish ministry. He will feel rejected and hurt and unloved. He may develop physical symptoms and begin to suffer emotionally and mentally. He may lash out in anger and attack his members openly or subtly. He may withdraw into his study and sulk. He may become depressed and beaten down.

None of these reactions will be helpful if the minister is committed to helping a group of Christians become agents of reconciliation in God's world. He will have to become involved in the conflict and deal with it. He will have to admit his own hostility, learn how to accept it, and deal with it. In preaching, teaching, counseling, he will have to help his congregation look at their hostility toward him and other members of the church.

Members of the church will have to learn how to become angry with each other, furiously angry, admit it, talk about it, and still be able to love each other in the midst of disagreement.

CREATIVE CONFLICT

Conflict cannot be avoided in a church that seriously involves itself in God's world. But conflict can be creative if it is recognized and brought out in the open.

We learned this from the controversy stirred up by the Vietnam forums. The rejection and hostility released by that encounter was threatening. It drove us to look at our theological assumptions about what is sacred and what is secular. Within two years this conflict produced the long-range planning study described in Chapter 4. The conflict caused by the forums contributed to our defining as a church what we were trying to be and do in God's world.

A more immediate fruit of that conflict was the reconstruction of our entire adult education program. The inability of many of our members to know what God was doing in the world and what we were about as a church led us to bring forth a program to educate ourselves about God's world and man's role in it.

The tension which the forum produced in me changed my whole style of thinking and strategy as well as upset me emotionally. I sought out a conference at Princeton Seminary on how to live in freedom in this technological age and found new direction. I spent two weeks at the Institute for Advanced Pastoral Studies in Bloomfield Hills, Michigan, where I was helped to examine my emotional upheaval. However, these conferences were not enough. I found a counselor who helped me to understand, to accept, and to deal with my feelings of anxiety and hostility which conflict in the congregation raised in me. Over the past six years he has helped me to face conflict and live through it somewhat constructively.

Each time another family left the church I had the old anxious feelings and inner tensions. My personal experiences have helped me to accept and to understand some of the feelings our members have when they have felt rejection.

When we voted to give $15,000 from the King Fund to the Welfare Rights Organization of Philadelphia to organize those on welfare into some kind of power base, the issue was hotly debated. The vote to give the money barely passed. On the way out of the meeting, a person who had made a speech against the grant heard a fellow member say, "Well, when we get rid of those who voted against it, we'll have a good church." The person who made the negative speech felt outside the fellowship and considered separating himself from the church.

I heard about this incident. The next week we were dealing with conflict at board meetings, and I cited this instance as an example of how we must learn to deal with hostility and forgive each other. When the rejected member spoke up and admitted it happened to him, we asked him to express his feelings. He did so at some length. We dealt with the issue and out of it came a surge of acceptance and love. He could be against the grant for welfare rights and still be received and loved by those who opposed him.

People in churches have not learned how to face conflict and deal with it. Bad feelings are shared at the Sunday dinner table, or spread through the church by telephone. Seldom do churches develop a plan to get at hostility and confront it openly.

For seven years, dealing with hostility and anger brought about by different views of how we should perform the mission of Jesus Christ has been one of my primary occupations. I have spent hours with men at luncheon tables in Philadelphia trying to reconcile views and to keep people together. I have met with couples and talked into the night, getting at feelings we have about our theological convictions. Many times, both ministers of the church have gone together to attempt an understanding, to listen and to be reconciled.

During the antiballistic missile debate it became clear that I was opposed to spending money for this system when human needs were so pressing. A member of the congregation has served in the United States Army as a career. We were on opposite sides of the issue. One day we were talking and his wife said, "How do you feel about the church getting part of our tithe money? It comes from an army pension and is part of the defense budget." This question opened up a feeling level of sharing which we had never had before. I said, "You should be able to say to me, 'We disagree with you strongly on your view of the ABM system. We will fight you on it to the end.' I should be able to say that I disagree violently with you. However, we should still be able to love each other and be in the same church."

TWO VIEWS OF THE CHURCH

Much of the conflict which arises when a church attempts to change comes from two opposing views of the church held by members who often attend the same local church.

One group, composed largely of people born in the early 1900's, sees the church as a place to find peace of mind, as a place to come on Sunday morning to get their spiritual batteries recharged. "Come unto me all ye who labor and are heavy laden and I will give you rest," is a favorite text. Old familiar hymns are loved best, like "In the Garden," where "He walks with me and talks with me and tells me I am His own."

I can appreciate this view. These people have gone through two ghastly world wars and a devastating depression, as well as the Korean War, the advent of the A-bomb, and the whole struggle of social revolution we are in today. They see the world shaking and want the church to be the rock to which they can cling.

Another group sees the role of the church as a catalytic agent to bring change in a world full of injustice, evil, and sin. The church is a launching pad to fire the rocket of freedom and liberty for all Americans into orbit. Their favorite text is, "except a man lose his life he cannot find it." Amos and Hosea are their models. The revolutionary Christ taking on the religious establishment and challenging governmental leaders to be just is their man for today. They see the gospel of the cross as calling them to be involved radically in all of life, and as they lose their lives in servant living, they will find the fruits of the Spirit, peace and joy.

The man who wrote me when the National Council voted to admit Red China to the United Nations, "That's the last straw. I just can't belong to a church that talks like that," obviously belongs to those who hold the first world view. So does the woman who said, "My husband gets involved with blacks all week, and we don't want to hear anything about that on Sunday."

How can people committed to these two world views live and work together in the same congregation? Some of them cannot. The two world views can easily cause rigidity and dogmatism in a congregation. If those committed to the first view dominate a church, those who hold the second will become frustrated and discouraged about the church ever coming alive. If those committed to the second view control the church, they can become arrogant and impatient with those who disagree with them.

We have seen about forty families leave our church for one reason or another. I believe the basic reason is always the same, a disagreement about what the mission of the church is in the world, and a disagreement about how that mission is to be accomplished.

With some people who left there was never a chance for dialogue. They simply went out at the first threat and closed the door. Some went to other churches —

most to a church that was more comfortable and less threatening. Some have simply dropped out of the church altogether. Some spend their weekends at the cottage, skiing, or playing golf.

However, as our church has gone from one style of ministry to another, many persons under age thirty, who had given up on the church, have come around to see what is going on. The year we voted the Martin Luther King, Jr., Memorial Fund of $100,000, we received ninety new members, nearly all knowing what kind of church they were getting into and coming for that reason. In the middle of one crisis period, a former Roman Catholic came to the church and said, "Can you use me?" We could and did.

I believe that the style of mission involvement in God's world caused many of our members to ask for the first time, "Do I really believe that is what the gospel says? Is this the kind of church I want? Is this what Christian discipleship means? Does Jesus want this from me?" For the first time they heard the radical call of Jesus to leave all and follow him.

THE MINISTER AND CONFLICT

Clergymen are a group of people who, on the whole, seem to need a lot of acceptance and love. A man may choose the ministry because his relation to a congregation will provide him with support, attention, and a feeling of being needed. The ministry has been built on the premise that a clergyman will talk and act so as to make his parishioners happy and satisfied. This assumption puts him in an impossible bind. How is a man going to be loved and lauded when he calls for action which threatens every fiber in his parishioners'

beings? Whether the issue concerns black-white relations or the war in Vietnam, it does not matter. Any
minister today who preaches and lives a biblical theology of involvement in God's world is going to raise a
lot of anger in the church he serves. Few ministers are
emotionally equipped to take the flak.

It is easier to not discover a biblical theology which
demands radical discipleship. No one will ever attack
a man or reject him for saying, "Lord, Lord." A minister can rationalize away any discipleship call which
says, "Leave all and come follow me."

A preacher can "stick to the Bible" and leave his
application in the first century or make the application
on a personal, pious level, and come out of the pulpit
to receive platitudes at the door. He can skillfully
avoid dealing with anything that is controversial and
have a long pastorate in a quiet and often dying situation. He can count his members and look at his budget
and believe that the church is alive and vital. However,
in his heart, he knows the call of Jesus to Peter, James,
and John and to him, to "leave the nets and come,"
has never been received. He knows in his heart that he
is like the rich young ruler — a phony.

CONFLICT THAT MATTERS

In an article in the *Saturday Review*, September 6,
1969, Richard Farson made a plea for those in institutions to raise the level or quality of discontent. Let us
have discontent in the church about issues that really
matter.

I visited a church where the issue was whether the
young people should dance in the parish house. The
minister wondered if he should go out on a limb in

support. My first inclination was to say, "Forget it, if that's the key issue the place is already dead. Look for another church or another occupation."

Does God care whether young people dance in the parish house? God cares terribly about whether we go on developing bacterial war to let loose on our enemies. God cares terribly about whether we go on polluting our air and water. But dancing in the parish house!

Another church I visited was uptight over whether people should be allowed to join a Baptist church without immersion. In a world where we are spending $80 billion on arms and beginning to deploy anti-ballistic missile sites against the Russians and Chinese, why any church would bother one second about baptism by immersion confuses me. If missiles begin to fly across the polar ice caps, immersion will be in death.

Many of the petty housekeeping duties which ministers do and which they ask important laymen to give time to perform are sheer nonsense. Much of what goes on inside a church in the name of God is totally unimportant. It keeps people coming around the church, keeps them busy, keeps them dependent, and prevents them from any sort of meaningful Christian discipleship.

It is past time for the people of God to stop "playing church" on Sunday morning at 11:00 A.M. and begin to face the issues of controversy and conflict in our world; such as, prison reform, crime and justice, the ending of the war in Vietnam, alleviation of racial strife, purification of air and water resources, and the feeding of the poor.

My feelings in the past led me to avoid conflict situations. I tried to calm angry members down, call a halt, maintain the status quo, and hope that everything would return to normal. I have learned that such a flight tactic will never solve the problem of hostility. The minister has got to face his own hostility first of all and deal with it. He has got to face his own vocational call and decide what it means to be a disciple of Jesus Christ in a fearful and terrible, but potentially beautiful, world. Then he will have to help those with whom he works to face their anger and channel the anger-power into constructive action for the survival of man on this earth.

There can be love in conflict. A people can love a minister and work with him while being angry about what he does and says. A minister can love people who are his enemies, the members of his own congregation. Ministers and people can learn to use hostility to fight evil. Anger can be the motive power to drive a church in working for the kingdom of God on earth. When anger and love are understood, lived with, and used in a people whom God has called together, constructive action which is authentic can begin to take place.

9. Risks and Results of Change

Conflict is not the only result of change in a church. There is also the danger of potential damage to the church's "success" image, which has traditionally been measured in terms of membership rolls and budget.

LOSS OF MEMBERS

A church which becomes involved in issues which are controversial will lose members. One Sunday in 1960 a black family came forward during worship to take the first step in joining our congregation. I had just reached home when a member phoned to say, "You're not going to take them in are you?" When I assured him that the board of deacons had already discussed the matter and voted to receive anyone who came to join our fellowship, he replied, "You will lose members. You will lose money."

When a minister gets caught in the middle of issues like this, he will be timid and easily threatened. From the start, it is important that he have support of groups and committees for his action. He would be wise not to get caught out alone on an issue limb. In the above case the deacons had already considered what would happen if black people came to join our congregation. In that meeting of the deacons, the issue was not settled until a deacon who was born in Georgia said, "Of course we must receive any person who comes. It is the Christian action and we must do it." Later on, when we faced the war issue and civil rights decisions, the member who phoned me left our congregation. He joined a church which was not so immersed in the life of God's world.

Different people have different threat levels. Some will flee a church when that church takes a simple step toward involvement. The first time a group departed from our church was during the controversy over the forums on the war. About a dozen families refused to pledge for the budget that year and began to absent themselves from worship. Since that time most of them have joined other churches or dropped out.

Since then, each time we have become embroiled in a controversial issue that produced a crisis, there has been a loss of members. Some have gone away quietly. Some have tried to rally support for their position by calling other members.

The morning in April, 1968, when we voted on the Martin Luther King, Jr., Memorial Fund, nearly every member who was committed to the view that the church exists to be a comfort station was present. However, we had been working through education, planning, and preaching for several years and had won the support of the majority of our members to a theological conviction that the church exists for mission in the world. Those who were against mortgaging the church and giving the money for ministry in the urban crisis lost. Since then, many of them have dropped out, even after consistent dialogue urging them to stay and present their viewpoint.

I have always believed that the church exists to take

the call of discipleship for Jesus seriously. Until I came to Wayne I had never worked with a group of people who were willing to risk much. "Relax and enjoy life. You'll live longer and you won't get an ulcer," one senior clergyman told me.

However, the story of Gideon always came to mind. He asked for volunteers to go against the Midianites. Thirty-two thousand came forward. Gideon said, "Everyone who is afraid, go home." Twenty-two thousand returned home. The remaining group he ran through a stream. All who laid on their stomachs to drink he sent back. Those who lapped the water on the run he recruited. There were three hundred. This seems to be the way any church will move when it begins to be involved in servant ministry in God's world.

In the long run, fewer members will bring about more change, for they will be dedicated. They will be action-reflection type people who will have drive and passion to be radical servants for Jesus Christ in the world. No member should be allowed to drop out of a church until every effort is made to communicate with him and to love him. Nonetheless, once a minister and a group of people decide that they exist for mission in God's world, then nothing should deter them from acting on this theological assumption.

To be free to lose members requires a people who can sit loose with the institutional church. When a hundred passionate followers become more important than a thousand fringe-benefit Christians who come around on Christmas and Easter, then a church is loose to the idea that keeping the institution going is the most important thing. This church has discovered discipleship is measured by commitment, not by numbers.

CONFLICT AND GIVING

During the turmoil of the Vietnam forums, which came in the midst of our fall attempt to raise the budget for the next year, a member came into my office and threw down a dozen pledge cards. He said, "None of these people will pledge because of the Vietnam thing." He probably expected me to feel threatened, which I was. At the time, my feeling about his nonverbal message was, "You had better watch out what you are doing in this church or you will be out."

I had always believed that a crisis at the time pledges were being taken was a bad thing. Two responses changed my mind. One loyal family heard about the twelve cards and said, "Every dollar we lose because of the forums, we will make up." It was not necessary for them to do so. A new family came to join our church because of the church's willingness to risk. Their opening pledge made up for the twelve lost pledges. That fall the church budget went from $82,000 to $85,000. The next year, when we were in another period of conflict, the budget increased to $92,500.

The proposition that facing conflict will raise the church budget will not be true for all congregations. Churches have taken bold stands in the name of servant ministry and suffered grave loss of funds. It has become standard practice for church members who disagree with the style of ministry pursued by a clergyman to punish him by withdrawing financial support.

This withholding of gifts has happened in Central Baptist each time the church has become involved in a "sticky issue." However, other members have come forward with increased support, or new members have appeared to make up for the losses.

A person finds it natural not to support an institution or a ministry to which he is opposed. My statement from the beginning to members who disagree has been: "A couple do not separate and file for divorce at the first big argument; so why should you divorce the church from your financial support at the first big disagreement of how we are to be servant ministers of Jesus Christ?"

One reason why we did not suffer more financial loss as the involvements in the city, in civil rights, in the Martin Luther King, Jr., Memorial Fund developed was six years of small-group ministry, where a fourth of the congregation had been meeting in homes to read theology and learn what it meant to be the church. This hard core stood by with courage and moved with insight. Also several years of pastoral care and calling had built up a relationship with people that was able to weather some severe storms.

To the credit of many members who had been in the church for many years, and who may not have been in sympathy with the way the church was changing its style of ministry, they stayed in the church with a spirit of Christian love and even increased their support.

With the general tenor of a decrease in church attendance in America, the advance of the secular age, the alienation of the young from organized Christianity, churches have felt the squeeze on their budgets. It is commonplace for churches to fall short of proposed budgets. Denominational agencies are cutting back drastically. The years ahead are going to be tough years for raising money to support church budgets and denominational programs. A recent Gallup poll shows church attendance falling from 49 percent of the nation's adults attending church on a typical Sunday, to 42 percent by 1968. The average attendance for the 21-29 year old group is 33 percent. The trend of people coming to worship is downward.

Thus far, this trend has not been the case for Central. The average attendance at worship for the year runs around 75 percent of the membership. Our budget has risen from $57,000 in 1960 to $115,000 in 1971. This increase was not due to a great influx of new families. There were 190 families in 1960 and 230 in 1969. The yearly budget is not the whole story of giving either. In addition to what we give for current expenses and missionary work, the congregation pledged $57,000 in March, 1968, for the World Mission Campaign of the American Baptist Convention (to be paid in three years), took on the Martin Luther King, Jr., Memorial Fund in April, 1968, for $100,000, and bought an organ for $35,000. (See Appendix 7 for an analysis of membership and giving trends in the church. Appendix 6 contains an annotated list of all of the projects aided by the King Fund.)

PLANNING FOR RESPONSE

Responsible giving of the financial resources of a congregation is the result of pastoral care and counseling, a theology of action embedded in a Christian people, an educational program which informs the congregation about the world we live in, dialogical and interpretive preaching about what God is doing in the world, worship which celebrates what God is doing through the church, and careful planning for servant ministry in the world.

This statement says that the raising of church budgets

in most churches ten or twenty years from now will depend on whether the present generation is convinced about putting its money in church institutions. Many of the young will not be convinced at all about the church and will write it off. However, many young people can be reached. Fifty couples under thirty have joined in the ministry of Central in the last two years because they were convinced that a church in mission outside its walls could be effective in bringing change to society.

At the present time, congregations across the United States are full of aging persons who give money to raise church budgets. In twenty years many of the people who now control the style of status-quo ministry found in American churches will be gone. Unless the church begins now to develop an open style of servant living and risk, there will not be many around to carry on budgets.

RESULTS OF CHANGE

On Tuesday morning, April 23, 1968, a letter came to the church office on a yellow piece of paper. It said, "I read the account concerning you in the morning paper. For a few days now I have been looking to the Lord for direction in sending my monetary blessings, my gratitude to God for allowing me [sic], and providing employment with increase and direction. My name is fictitious, but not my Spirit. Use the money to His Glory — The King Fund: He who is King of Kings and Lord of Lords. Thank you for allowing this act of yours to be printed." Enclosed in the letter was ninety dollars in five and ten dollar bills.

The account referred to in this letter was an article

which appeared in *The Philadelphia Inquirer* on April 22, 1968, under the heading "Church OKs Mortgage to Aid City Poor." The news item went on to say: "Members of a Baptist congregation in suburban Wayne voted overwhelmingly Sunday to mortgage their church to help finance a $100,000 Martin Luther King, Jr., Memorial Fund 'to meet the human needs in the Philadelphia area.' "

The fact that this action of our church was "news" indicates how little is really expected of the church today.

In June, 1968, *The Philadelphia Evening Bulletin* ran an editorial under the heading, "One Church's Bridge Building." It said,

An uneasiness has been spreading in the suburbs in the wake of the Kerner Commission report, made more intense by the assassination of Dr. Martin Luther King, Jr. The isolation that many sought in green suburbia now begins to look like a moat separating residents there from efforts to deal with the nation's grinding urban problems.

The moat, however, can be bridged. And one does not have to wait for the apparatus of government to lower the span. Individuals, groups, churches can do it themselves, a notable example being recent action by the relatively small and not very affluent Central Baptist Church in Wayne.

A couple of weeks ago a quorum of its 375 adult members got together and voted to borrow in the church's name—mortgage or other loan—$100,000 to be used to meet "the most pressing human needs" in the urban area.

The church is still collecting ideas on how to spend the money. One likely use is construction of ten housing units for low-income families on six acres of land the church has near Paoli.

Or some of the money may go to further the work of the Ludlow Home Improvement Corp. in the area near Temple University. The church and the Ludlow Community Association joined in organizing the home improvement group, and the involvement has led to other things for Central Baptist members—helping set up a thrift shop in the neighborhood, teaching, work with Scouts.

These efforts by themselves are not going to solve the urban problem, as the Rev. Richard Keach, Central Baptist's pastor, is well aware. "It's a token," he says, "a sign of involvement. Will the church come out? If 100 churches do the same, it would be something sizable. I've always thought that the secret of helping the city is getting the suburbs involved with it."

The yield will be in human terms, but the commitment of money makes it "for real." Central Baptist is offering leadership where it is needed.

All of this flurry of publicity without our solicitation, after the initial story was released, convinced us that news of action by the church is so rare that the mass media will come eagerly to use any hopeful sign that the church can and will still act in the name of the gospel of helping and healing that it so often talks about.

The King Fund stimulated great interest from many church groups. The ministers and leaders of the church have made speeches and presentations everywhere from New Jersey to Kansas. Many churches continue to ask: "Do you have someone who could come to our church and help us get our church free so that we may become involved?"

At this moment the present Fund Committee is organizing and training groups of lay people to go to churches, help them develop a plan and find a way to move and organize for servant ministry.

Our church is located on the borders of a great metropolitan area which has all the growing problems of the big cities of America. Any congregation, whether it is located in the city, on the borders of the city, or in the

46521

rural areas, can be involved in "the most pressing human needs" which it sees around it.

Unfortunately, it is difficult to persuade a congregation to want to see the needs that lie on its doorstep. Churches have not considered it to be their responsibility to be involved in the "great" problems of America. They have considered their ministry to be to those who come into their buildings. The task has been to educate, train, teach, reach, and save. All these ministries we accept as basic.

The theological premise of this book is that when the person has been reached, won into the fellowship of God called the church, then the real task of ministry begins.

Appendix 1
Central Baptist Involvement

CENTRAL BAPTIST CHURCH
Wayne, Pennsylvania*

15 miles west of Philadelphia on Route 30
425 members, 238 families
draw from 15-mile radius
estimated family income—$12,600
current giving:

budget	$100,000	($32,000 benevolences)
World Mission Campaign	20,000	
MLK Fund	12,000	
Total	$132,000	

CENTRAL BAPTIST CHURCH INVOLVEMENT

REFLECTION	ACTION	RESEARCH
Study Groups	Mission Giving—47%	N. Philadelphia Research Project
Sunday 9:30—11:00 A.M. 4-6 classes 125 average involved	Refugee Resettlement (5 families to date)	Field Trips
	International Christian Youth Exchange (ICYE)	Task Forces Public Education Police Relations Problem Pregnancies Prison Reform
Monthly (evenings) 6-9 groups 100 average involved	Fair Housing Programs	
Open Forums	Ludlow—N. Philadelphia Ludlow Housing Improvement Corporation	Strategic Planning Process
Vietnam ABM Abortion Welfare Rights Draft Dissent	Sewing Classes Thrift Shop	Sensitivity Training Action-Research Training (Minister of Education)

*This document was prepared by Bruce Copeland for a conference of the National Council of Churches at Indianapolis, Indiana, in July, 1969.

MLK Fund Project Reports	Main Line Housing Improvement Corporation
Experimental Worship	MLK Fund—$100,000 12 projects
Communion Breakfast Youth Led Worship Moments of Concern	Work with Alienated Youth
Hearings	Integrated Nursery School
Kerner Commission Report Black Manifesto	Crafts of Freedom Shop
	Tutorial Projects

CENTRAL BAPTIST CHURCH INVOLVEMENT

1961—Beginning of sponsoring International Christian Youth Exchange students

1964—Beginning of Central Baptist Nursery School for the community

1964—Sponsoring of the first Cuban refugee family

1965—Youth ministry to the community begun

1965—Community forum on Vietnam war

1966—Task force formed out of which came Ludlow Housing Improvement Corporation

1966—Adult education classes started

1967—Long-range strategic plan study made

1967—Main Line Community Association formed

1967—Crafts of Freedom Shop opened (a craft shop which sells goods made by people in Appalachia, all profits going to people in that area)

1968—Formation of thrift shop in Ludlow

1968—World Mission Crusade. Central Baptist pledged $56,373.

1968, April—Central voted the Martin Luther King, Jr., $100,000 Urban Crisis Fund

1969, May—Community meeting on the Antiballistic Missile System

1969—Beginning of Lay Ministry Task Force Program in Wayne

1969, October—Opening of the Wayne Community Youth Center

1969—Formation of the Philadelphia Clergy Consultation Service on Problem Pregnancies

1970—Reorganization of the church boards for mission

1971—Beginning of Lay Ministry Training Program

1971—Crafts of Freedom Shop opened daily all year

Appendix 2
Strategic-Planning Document

PURPOSE OF THE CENTRAL BAPTIST CHURCH

The purpose of the Central Baptist Church of Wayne is to witness fearlessly to all persons that Jesus Christ as Lord and Savior is in the midst of human life calling us to decision and to make responsible use of our human and material resources. We are to be God's servants in the places where we work and spend our days. Our purpose for gathering for worship, study, planning, and in all our groups is to celebrate God's presence in the world and to plan for mission. These experiences free us to love boldly, and to be involved responsibly as persons and as an institution in all of life.

I. UNDERLYING ASSUMPTIONS

A. Theological Assumptions

1. God and World

God's concern and interest is with all aspects of human life and activity, personal and group relationships, structures and nature. God's concern is all that which traditionally has been known as secular and sacred.

As persons we have been freed through the death and resurrection of Jesus Christ to move out into the world's needs, challenging the status quo where it involves social inequities and evils, pointing out to men in their world the redeeming, affirming love of God. This love frees men to participate fully in the drama of life.

2. Mission

Mission is God's work of actively engaging men in his design and purpose. By design and purpose we mean:

Acceptance of Christ's lordship which leads to the discovery and proclamation of a new world order in which men live for each other.

Reconciliation between hostile people.

Taking responsibility for God's world and people.

Confrontation of those institutions and structures in our community which dehumanize and break peoples' lives; addressing those institutions and structures and calling them to responsible thought and action.

3. The Church

The church is to be a sign and a symbol of the truth that God has brought healing and hope to all men. It is to be the living sign of the fact that when men are caught up by God's love and forgiveness, they move out in love and forgiveness to others (mission). The church is to provide a sustaining and supporting fellowship for persons so that they can grow spiritually to the end that they live out their lives as Christ's servants in the world and abide in hope. The church seeks to fulfill these purposes when it:

Witnesses to all men that God loves them and desires them to be his servants.

Demonstrates in action the fact that God loves all men, those within the church and those without.

Sensitizes itself to the conflicts of life in the local community as well as the entire world.

Gives itself to all people including the hostile, alienated, and broken.

Celebrates through worship the victory and truth of God's triumph over the powers of alienation, bigotry, and self-centeredness.

Surrounds, supports, and inspires persons to engage in ministry without regard to personal sacrifice.

4. The Ministry

All persons who accept baptism and membership take upon themselves the ministry of Jesus Christ. Therefore, church membership means ministry.

The ministry takes its shape around the human needs of men everywhere. Ministry is giving oneself up to the needs of people with the assurance that God is with us in every area of life.

Ministry includes the relating of the story of God's work through Jesus Christ and the calling of persons to respond in faith and love.

B. Sociological Assumptions

1. Education

In a highly technical and specialized society, the demands on educational institutions will become more complex and reveal the inadequacies of structure and educational philosophy. We in the church, as we take both public and Christian education seriously, are becoming more keenly aware that they are inextricably bound together.

2. Families

The complexities of our society will continue to put new pressures on the family with the likelihood of an increase of mental illness, emotional deprivation, divorce, and crime.

3. Government and Politics

The government is playing an increasing role in our lives, requiring the development of responsible political participation on the part of all citizens in order that government may serve the needs of all people.

4. Housing

There is a desperate need for new and rehabilitated housing in both the city and suburbs for those who presently live in deprived conditions.

5. Peace

The prevention of war and the establishment of a durable peace with justice and freedom is an overriding issue of our time. As Jesus came to reconcile the world to himself, so must his followers be agents of reconciliation in a tense and fearful world.

6. Poverty

In spite of present programs developed to alleviate poverty for one-fifth of our population, the flight of industry from the city, the overloading of welfare agencies, the outworn concepts of welfare, the continuance of inflation, and the replacement of blue collar jobs point to the need for new and creative programs of job retraining, services to the aged, and help for those who are unemployed.

7. Race

Present evidence points to a hardening of racial lines in the suburbs and cities with the expansion of the ghetto.

II. OBJECTIVES

A. Lay Ministry

We will develop a training program for lay ministry to witness to the redeeming and reconciling love of God in their ministry to each other and to all men.

We will develop a training program for lay ministry in the vocations and institutions in which all are involved.

B. Worship and Life

Through thoughtful study and experimentation we will strive to more effectively integrate the issues and concerns of our daily work with the way we celebrate on Sunday morning and other occasions, in order that our work may truly be an extension and expression of our worship, and our worship the offering up of our work.

C. Corporate Ministry

We will continue to develop the church's agenda for corporate ministry around the most pressing needs of our world in which we can responsibly and effectively become involved.

D. Christian Education

We will provide structures and relationships in which children, youth, and adults will be helped to grow spiritually and be trained to think theologically about how God is acting in the lives of persons, institutions, and events through:

Disciplined study of the historical and biblical roots of faith.

Exposure to the realities and needs of our world.

E. Use of Human and Material Resources

Being aware that our human and material resources are a trust from God, we will use our material wealth—money, buildings, time—to meet human needs.

Appendix 3
Adult Education Curriculum

ADULT CLASSES FROM SEPTEMBER, 1966 THROUGH 1969

September to October 30, 1966—Classes listed on page 25

November 6—December 18, 1966

1. Biblical Theology in a Revolutionary Age
   To find a style of Christian life which is authentic for a revolutionary time.
2. The Prevention and Care of Family Crises
   The course was taught by a doctor-psychologist and dealt with mental health in the family.
3. The Gospel of John
   An introduction and interpretation of John.
4. Uniform Lesson Series
   This quarter on Isaiah and Jeremiah.
5. Vietnam
   Vital issues in the great debate led by a political science teacher.

January 8—March 19, 1967

1. Child Behavior in the Formative Years
   A study of the preschool child for parents, taught by a psychologist member of the church.
2. The Ecumenical Scandal
   A study of the ecumenical movement, led by a member of the congregation.
3. Seminar on City Problems
   A discussion of the problems of housing, jobs, and education in the city of Philadelphia, led by a former member of the city planning board.
4. Uniform Lesson Series
   A study in Luke.
5. Vietnam
   Continuation of last quarter.

April 2—June 11, 1967

1. Uniform Lesson Series
   The story of the early church in the book of Acts.

2. Issues Confronting Parents

An exploration of the issues confronting parents in this day, including mass media, value systems, identity, and the generation spread. Leaders from the community were brought in each week.

3. Contemporary South and Southeast Asia

A survey of the political problems of this area of the world. Attention was given to Hinduism, Buddhism, and Islam. The course was taught by a political science teacher.

4. The Converted Church

A study of the message and mission of the church in this age.

September 10—November 12, 1967

1. Living with Your Adolescent

This course repeated the course offered in the fall of 1966.

2. Jewish-Christian Dialogue

Jewish rabbis, teachers, musicians visited the class and spoke of the American Jew in the twentieth century.

3. The World and Worship

The forms of worship and the meaning of worship were explored. The whole question of worship in a secular age was considered.

4. Uniform Lesson Series

Continuation of the study of the book of Acts.

5. Interpersonal Discussion Group

A group of people met the entire church school year to search for what it means to be an authentic person. The seminar was led by a professor of pastoral theology.

November 26—December 30, 1967

1. Catholic-Protestant Relations

Catholic priests, nuns, and teachers presented the struggle for reform going on in the Roman Catholic church today.

2. Biblical Studies in the Uniform Lesson Series

3. City and Suburb

An examination of the ways in which the city and suburban community can work together in mission.

4. Abortion: Dilemma and the Law

The question of abortion was studied. Speakers were invited in and the class participated in a Philadelphia station television presentation which came from the class, dealing with the issue of abortion.

January 7—March 24, 1968

 1. Civil Disobedience
    Leaders were invited to speak to the class about the place of nonviolent civil disobedience as a tactic for action in the world today.
 2. The Mission and Purpose of Central Baptist
    This class was the regular membership class for all new members.
 3. Uniform Lessons
    A study of biblical material taught by laymen of the church.
 4. Film Forum
    Films were shown and discussed which had to do with the Christian message.

April 21—June 9, 1968

 1. The Meaning of Sexuality
    A psychiatrist led a class for youth and adults on maleness and femaleness, seeking to help the class members discover the real self.
 2. Joy to the World
    A class which looked at the hope theme in worship and prepared a service of worship for the entire congregation.
 3. A Time to Listen, A Time to Act
    The U.S. Commission Report on Civil Rights was studied. A leader in community planning from Philadelphia led the class.
 4. Studies in the Old Testament
    The books of Job, Proverbs, and Ecclesiastes.

September 15—November 3, 1968

 1. The Church in the World
    The new members class for adults.
 2. Studies of Writings in Faith
    The course included the books of Peter, Hebrews, John, and Revelation and was led by two members of the church.
 3. How Children Learn
    Two nursery teachers led this course on how children learn. The course was for both mothers and fathers.
 4. Power and Justice
    A worker-priest from Philadelphia taught the course on the church, political power, black power, and justice.

November 17, 1968—January 12, 1969

 1. Biblical Studies in the New Testament

A layman continued the study of the last quarter in the books of Revelation, John, and Mark.

2. The Punishment of Crime
   Leaders working in the field of crime were brought in to look at the trial and treatment of persons in the jails and prisons of Pennsylvania.

3. Education—A Look at a Changing Process
   Leaders from Temple University led a course on the educational models needed for this new time. Superintendents of the local high schools also spoke to the class.

4. Meaning of Faith in a New Age
   This class concerned itself with how the Christian faith relates itself to the issues of the day.

January 26—March 30, 1969

1. The Welfare Question
   Leaders from the Welfare Rights Organization of Philadelphia helped the class members to be informed about the welfare system in America, as well as poverty in the city.

2. Psychological Principles of Teaching
   Two members of the church led this class on the small-group process and teaching methods. The course was offered for those who wished to teach in our church school.

3. Personal Faith and Growth
   The class became a sensitivity group to explore the issues of faith and belief.

4. Studies in the Gospel of Mark, Uniform Lesson Series.

5. Love and Marriage
   The two ministers led a class for young married couples, dealing with issues which newly marrieds encounter.

April 20—June 8, 1969

1. American Militarism
   The whole issue of the military culture in the country was examined. The ABM system was also examined.

2. Biblical Study
   A biblical study of the meaning of revelation, inspiration, and authority, as well as how to understand the Bible.

3. Purpose and Ministry of the Church
   The class for all new members.

4. Living Together—Explorations in Communications
   Through the use of role playing and small-group involvement, the group explored the meaning of living together as persons.

September 8—December 1, 1969

1. Four Seminars on Components of the Black Revolution
   Four different groups, led by black members of the church and community, analyzed the issues of the black revolution going on in America.
2. The Book of Samuel
   A study of the book of Samuel with the minister, with the class discussing the sermons preached each Sunday from First Samuel and helping to explore the passage for the next one.

REQUIRED CLASS FOR ALL NEW ADULT MEMBERS

Curriculum

Session 1—The World Come of Age

A discussion of the concept put forth by Dietrich Bonhoeffer that we are in a new and radical age demanding a new and radical theology. Questions presented: What are the key issues that you see facing the Christian and the church today? What has happened in our world? What does it mean to say that man has come of age? How does a man grow up? Biblical models of Moses, Amos, Jacob, and Jesus are used.

Session 2—Religionless Christianity

Members of the class bring in reports on questions, such as: How do we move to maturity? What makes for change? How have you changed? How can we help people stay open to the world they live in? Reports on these questions come from *Letters and Papers from Prison* by Bonhoeffer. Biblical models of people who stayed open in the Old and New Testaments are studied. The question of what kind of people can become involved in today's church is discussed.

Session 3—The Church in the World

A class member reports on *Where in the World?* by Colin Williams. A member of the church shares his plan on how his insurance company is doing the work of God in the world. The rest of the period is spent dealing with the form which the church will take in the secular world. The roles of the laity and clergy are discussed around the question: What will the church look like in twenty-five years?

Session 4—The Parable

The film *The Parable* is shown and discussed in terms of the servant concept of ministry.

Session 5—History of Central Baptist Church

Copeland presents where Central Baptist Church was ten years ago, where it is now, and what the struggle has been in the last years. We talk about what is needed to break open the church in order to make it free to be a servant in the life of the world.

Session 6—Baptism in the Baptist Tradition

Members of the class are asked to come prepared to discuss the meaning of symbols, particularly the symbol of baptism, liturgy, and those symbols used in worship. Using chapters three and four in *God's Revolution and Man's Responsibility* by Harvey Cox, this session is devoted to an honest look at worship, liturgy, and symbols.

Session 7—The Lord's Supper in Baptist Tradition

If the subject of baptism is not finished, it is continued in this session. Communion, as meaning being broken and poured out in servant living, is presented and discussed.

Session 8—The Strategic-Planning Process of Central Baptist

This session is devoted to a presentation and discussion of the strategic-planning document which appears in Appendix 2.

REQUIRED CLASS FOR ALL YOUNG PEOPLE

JOINING THE CHURCH

Typical Curriculum

Session 1—*The Parable*

The film *The Parable* is shown. The group is broken into small groups for a discussion of these questions: What is real community? Who carries on the ministry started by Jesus Christ? What is the servant ministry of Jesus in the film? Who are the persons toward whom mission is directed?

Sessions 2 and 3—The Historical Roots of Baptism

1. Moses at the Sea. The Exodus as a symbol of baptism.

   2. The Baptism of Jesus.
     a. Identification with the outcasts of society.
     b. Public proclamation of the beginning of his ministry.
     c. Dedication to the task of bringing change into human relationships.
   3. Paul. Being buried to sin and resurrected to new life.

Session 4—The World in Which We Live

Showing the film *Happy Birthday, Felisa*. This offers an opportunity to discuss war, racism, and poverty.

The concept of lay ministry as it relates to young people is presented.

Session 5—The Relation of Baptism to Ministry

These issues are presented in small-group discussions: (1) You are being asked to give your life to the ministry of Jesus Christ. (2) This is a community event. The members of the church participate in this event with you. (3) The style of your ministry will be shaped by two things, the issues of the day and the school in which you spend your time.

Session 6—Preparing for Baptism

The following matters are presented: The service of baptism is carefully explained. The vows of baptism are discussed. Sponsors are selected. (A sponsor is a friend in the church who remains a friend for at least a year.)

Appendix 4
Worship Materials

1. Prayers on Entering

Lord Jesus, think through my mind, speak through my lips, work through my hands, and love through my heart.

"Lord, make me an instrument of your peace. Where there is hatred, let me sow love" (St. Francis of Assisi).

Forgive my doubt, my anger, my pride. By thy mercy, abase me. By thy strictness, raise me up.

"Lord, thine the day, and I the day's" (Dag Hammarskjöld, *Markings*).

Create in me a clean heart, O God, and renew a right spirit within me.

O God, open us to receive, to see, to hear, to participate, to respond, to live.

I remember the cutting edge you lived on, Jesus. Get me back on my own cutting edge.

"Warm me, Jesus, so I can give out some real warmth to some other very cold people" (Malcolm Boyd, *Are You Running with Me, Jesus?*).

2. Preparatory Statements Used to Open Worship

December 7, 1969

> "Go tell it on the mountain
> Over the hills and everywhere . . .
> Go tell it on the mountain
> That Jesus Christ is born!"
>
> Go tell it at My Lai! Tell it in Helsinki!
> Go tell it at the Paris peace talks!
>
> Tell the world about Jesus! How he came to expose the evil that lives in every man!

November 30, 1969

Children and young people these days don't make much God-talk. They use words like "getting turned on," "groovy," and "being with it."

That's God-talk in biblical language. Moses was turned on about getting the Jews out of slavery. Gideon was "with it" in taking on the Midianites.

Joseph was a "groovy" person. The language is different. The subject is the same.

November 16, 1969

The machine is our friend and our enemy. It marches across the land mutilating the green hills, paving the valleys, fouling the sweet air, contaminating our waters. For this we get comfort and convenience. For this the nation's soul is being lost.

Again it is time to sing "America" and begin to fight, not only for liberty, but for "rocks and rills and templed hills," the trees, the breath, the water, the oceans!

This, too, is the mission of the church: God's people fighting for what God has created!

October 26, 1969

In this week's *Saturday Review*, Harvey Cox has an article "In Praise of Festivity." He appeals for a recovery of celebration of our festival days.

Today is Reformation Sunday, remembering October 31, 1517, when Martin Luther nailed the ninety-five theses on the door of the church at Wittenburg, Germany. Our worship today will celebrate Reformation!

October 5, 1969

Worship is celebration. All over the world—across the street with the Presbyterians, down the street with the Roman Catholics, people who call Jesus Lord are remembering and celebrating today—Worldwide Communion Sunday!

September 14, 1969

On Friday we watched the television program "The Death of Lake Erie." It asked the question: Is man polluting the air and water to such an extent that we are changing the balance of nature which may spell disaster for humans in America?

Worship is a time to consider the person and the soul, but also the world, the air, the water God has made, and to contemplate man's role in keeping it clean and pure.

3. Affirmations

Leader: There is a brother in me.
People: A brother to set me free.
Leader: I know it's there.
People: A brother to set my soul aflame.
Leader: If I can find his name
Unison: Let me find the brother, the brother in me.*

*Adapted from a song used in the TV documentary "A Time for Burning."

Leader: Jesus Christ is Lord of the world.
People: His lordship is over those who receive him and those who reject him.
Leader: Jesus Christ died for all persons.
People: He died for black and white, red and yellow people, of every race and creed.

Leader: Jesus Christ is Lord over the world.
People: His lordship is over insurance companies and the stock market.
Leader: Jesus Christ is Lord of all people.
People: He is for harassed businessmen, troubled parents, and dissenting youth.
Leader: Jesus Christ is Lord of this community.
People: We are salt and leaven and light to each other and to the world.

Leader: The kingdom of heaven is at hand.
People: The sick get well.
Leader: The lonely are visited.
People: The anxious find courage to live.
Leader: The dissenters become involved.
People: The fearful are able to love.

4. Prayers of Confession

We confess that we are a part of every man and every decision. We confess that we cannot be an island, but are part of mankind. We confess that we see the separation of parent and child. We confess that sometimes we "see it like it is, and sometimes like we wish it was." We confess that sometimes we cry, "Stop the world, I want to get off!" We confess to our failure to communicate across year barriers, color barriers, and nation barriers. God! You have a past and a future. You are showing us the past and calling us to live in reality in the future. Let the new come and begin with me.

Minister: Lord, hear our cry, our anxiety about our world, and forgive our separation.

Congregation: I am aware of your presence near me. In this worship I will seek to reach out to you in my thoughts, in my feelings, and in my silent prayers.

We confess that we live in a broken world and in a time of change and confusion. We confess that we are concerned about the safety of our families in the streets, and the conditions that produce violence in the streets. We confess that we must live together and communicate—black and white, Chinese and American, rich and poor—if we are to survive. We confess that we are concerned and care, but seem unable to move against such grave issues.

Minister: Enable us and empower us, ever living and loving God.

Congregation: God, help us to be and to do. Give us power to act in our schools, companies, and community.

Minister: Let us confess and ask forgiveness in silence.

We confess our deep desire for peace in Vietnam, for peace in our city streets, for peace in Israel, for peace in Biafra, for peace in our schools and colleges, for peace in ourselves.

Minister: Lord, enable us to be workers and makers of peace.

Congregation: May God help us to be a people of justice and love. May he give you power to be a healer. I pledge to you my time and concern as you live and make important decisions.

God, I confess how hard it is to be open to the conflicts in my life. I know I should be able to reject ideas without rejecting the person who expresses the idea. I cannot always do this and I'm frustrated by my inability to love rather than to hate, to confront rather than to ignore, to support rather than to ridicule, to forgive rather than to hold grudges. God, forgive my unwillingness to face these and other conflicts within myself.

Minister: There is neither Jew nor Greek, slave nor free, male nor female, for you are all one in Jesus Christ.

Congregation: If we confess our insensitiveness to each other, God will open us to each other. In silence let us ask for this.

5. Benedictions (Unison)

Now, Lord, let thou Thy servant depart in peace, according to Thy word. For my eyes have seen Thy salvation. Send me into the world again to live the life of the servant Christ. Strengthen my hand to serve, my mind to think, and my heart to respond to the needs of my fellow human beings.

God, I have come here for many reasons—to sing, to hear ideas, to just sit for an hour, because I feel I should come. Now it is time to go back to my routine. I hope I can live with more purpose because I have been here.

We leave with the conviction that we exist as a church for Your mission in the world. We take seriously Christ's call to be a servant in our work, in the schools of this area, in our political parties, and in the affairs of our nation that affect our world. Send us forth ready to respond and to care. And now, O Lord, let us depart in peace. Amen.

God! Help me to learn how to live with strife and hostility and find joy in the midst of pain. Help me to feel loved and to care deeply about other persons. Amen.

God, send us forth as healers and helpers of each other. Give us ears that listen, eyes that see, and wills that respond to human cries.

TYPICAL COMMUNION BREAKFAST

BEGINNING

Singing Around the Tables

Preparatory Statement

Affirmation

Leader: Jesus Christ is Lord of the world.
People: His lordship is over those who receive him and those who reject him.
Leader: Jesus Christ died for all persons.
People: He died for black and white, red and yellow people, of every race and creed.

Confession (Unison)

God, we confess our fear of letting go and trusting each other. We confess to feelings of smugness and superiority because of race, culture, and education. We confess our inability to reach out to persons who are sick, lonely, and dying. Bring us to these tables with an open eye, a hearing ear, a warm heart. Let there be a sense of oneness with all our Christian brothers.

Song: "Joy to the World"

THE HISTORICAL FAITH

Breaking and Sharing the Bread
Song: "Let Us Break Bread Together"
Eating Breakfast
Hearing the Scripture
Meditation on the Scripture
Concerns of the Congregation

Reception of New Members

Leader:	Do you desire to unite with this community?
Response:	I do.
Leader:	What do the members of this community offer these new members?
Community:	We extend our hands in welcome and support. We welcome you into a human community that seeks to be a sign and symbol of God's love for all men. We will support you as you live out your life as a minister of Jesus Christ in the world.
Leader:	Let us join together in a prayer of dedication.

Offering
Drinking the Cup

DEDICATION TO THE WORLD

Leader: "We've got some difficult days ahead. But it really doesn't matter with me now, because I've been to the mountaintop.

People: Like anybody, I would like to live a long life. But I'm not concerned about that now. I just want to do God's will.

Leader: And He's allowed me to go up to the mountain. And I've looked over and I've seen the promised land.

People: I may not get there with you, but I want you to know tonight that we as a people will get to the promised land."—Martin Luther King, April 3, 1968

Hymn of Dedication: "To Dream the Impossible Dream"

Benediction (Unison)
God, send us forth to declare to persons and institutions through our lives the impossible dream. Amen.

Appendix 5
Budget Planning

PROPOSED STRATEGIC-PLANNING BUDGET: CENTRAL BAPTIST CHURCH — 1970*

I. *Worship and Community Life*

Goal: We propose to integrate personal needs and commitments with corporate experiences of worship and fellowship so that members and friends of Central Baptist may discover a supporting fellowship of love and concern which celebrates in work and worship Christ's lordship over the whole world $29,765

Strategies:

1. Through a variety of methods and mediums to provide relevant and meaningful corporate services of worship $15,815

   a. music resources including music library, organ payments, maintenance, choir expenses, etc.   —$6,215
   b. music staff salaries   —$4,500
   c. one-quarter time of minister   —$5,000
   d. flowers   —$ 100

2. Through home visits, counseling, and small groups to provide support and encouragement for those in need and to deepen the Christian commitment of all $13,750

   a. one-half time of minister   —$10,000
   b. one-quarter time of minister of ed.—$ 3,750

3. Through church dinners and other fellowship occasions to encourage a spirit of common community .... $ 200

*Refer to Appendix 2 to see how this budget reflects the five implementing objectives of the Strategic-Planning Process.

II. *Christian Education*

Goal: We propose to provide structures and relationships in which children, youth, and adults will grow spiritually and be trained to think theologically about God acting in persons, institutions, and the world, through:

A. Providing an understanding of the Bible and the theological basis for faith in relationship to personal, family, and community experience.

B. Exposure to the realities and needs of our world as well as training for ministry in that world $22,450

Strategies:

1. Provide an expanded program of leadership education for teachers of children, youth, and adults in order to achieve our goal $4,000

2. Support of the goal through curriculum, publications, equipment, supplies, church library, and camps and conferences for teachers and participants .... $ 6,100

3. Undergird the preceding goals and programs with a Minister of Education (three-quarters of his time) $11,250

4. Continue the international youth exchange program .... $ 1,100

III. *Use of Material Resources*

Goal: Aware that our material resources are a trust from God, we propose to use these resources (money, buildings, and equipment) to meet human need. $40,075

Strategies:

1. We will maintain and administer essential services, property, and equipment $31,290

   a. utilities and fuel — $ 4,200
   b. insurance — $ 2,400
   c. repairs and maintenance — $ 3,705
   d. custodial services and supplies — $11,260
   e. miscellaneous — $ 725

f. office expense   —$ 2,300
g. secretary   —$ 3,700
h. one-eighth of minister's time   —$ 2,500
i. contingency   —$ 500

2. We propose to undertake a program of capital improvements .... $ 7,910

3. We propose to develop a more effective system for budget development, conducting the stewardship campaign, and disbursing funds .... $ 775

   a. canvass supplies   —$ 400
   b. financial supplies   —$ 375

4. We propose to begin a program of payment to Radnor Township for fire and police protection in lieu of taxes .... $ 100

IV. *Corporate Ministry*

Goal: We propose to further undergird and support the church's commitment to corporate ministry around the most pressing needs of our world in which we can responsibly and effectively become involved. $39,250

   Strategies:

1. We will support the home and world mission of the church through the varied ministries and programs of the A.B.C. ... $22,000

2. We propose to help support institutional ministries to children and youth in our metropolitan area .... $ 1,250

   a. Wayne Youth Project   —$ 200
   b. Inter-Church Child Care   —$ 100
   c. Baptist Home   —$ 475
   d. Baptist Children's House   —$ 475

3. We propose to help support institutional ministries to adults in our metropolitan area $11,600

   a. City missions   —$ 1,000
   b. MLK Fund   —10,000
      Interest —$5,000
      Principal—$5,000

     c. Wellsprings   —$ 200

     d. Eastern Campus Ministries   —$ 400

4. We propose to expose members of our congregation to community and world needs and to organize effective action to meet those needs .... $ 4,400

     a. Women's Fellowship program —$ 700

     b. Christian Social Concerns Committee —$ 1,000

     c. mission media —$ 200

     d. one-eighth of minister's time —$ 2,500

V. *Lay Ministry*

Goal: We propose to undertake an experimental program for lay ministry in order that men and women may be provided with the necessary resources and support for their ministry in and through the secular institutions of our society, especially where they are employed $15,100

Strategies:

1. Provide a full-time staff member to work with our laity and those of the wider community in the development of new models of support and resources for lay ministry $15,000

2. Share in support of Metropolitan Associates (an action-research project on lay ministry) which can bring resources to our program .... $ 100

Appendix 6
The Martin Luther King, Jr.,
Fund Report

THE MARTIN LUTHER KING, JR., FUND

From April, 1968, to January, 1969, the Central Baptist Church authorized the following expenditures for programs in the field of education, housing, and jobs for the Philadelphia area:

1. *Ludlow Summer Project* (1968), $5,350. Jointly sponsored by our fund, the Ludlow Community Association, and Temple Presbyterian Church, the project hired fourteen Ludlow area youth to work in summer recreation and voter registration, and to attend classes in black history.

2. *West Philadelphia Crime Prevention Association.* Our $10,000 grant has been used to sponsor an on-the-job training program centered at Mill Creek Community Center.

3. *West Philadelphia Opportunities Industrialization Center, Inc.,* $11,000. The fund's grant made possible the complete revision of the Electronics Training Program in West Philadelphia branch. The gift provided: a redesigned laboratory facility equipped with new work benches, the establishment of a special wire and soldering course designed to meet NASA specifications, and supportive testing equipment and individual student tools. By May, 1969, forty students had received training on the new equipment and twenty-two had been placed in jobs.

4. *Gate Library, Ardmore, Pa.,* $3,000. The Ardmore project was established as "a center where information on black history and culture would be made available to the public." Staffed by volunteers, Gate serves as a place for children to study and a resource to area schools in supplementing black history studies. (GATE stands for "Get Ahead Through Education.")

5. *Ellen Cushing Junior College,* Bryn Mawr, Pa., $5,000. This

unique school caters to the average student (those with high school records below the top 20 percent). About half of its students transfer, after the two-year program, into regular four-year colleges. The others benefit from the two-year program in terms of job skills, cultural development, and emotional maturity. Every dollar given by us has been matched with federal funds, making it possible for nine area black students to stay in school.

6. *Media Fellowship House*, Media, Pa., $15,000. Dedicated to "building a community free of racial, religious, and social tensions, through programs of social change," MFH has used most of our grant to employ job trainers and instructors for unemployed and underemployed persons. Training takes place at offices provided free by Boeing-Vertol. Trainees are paid traveling expenses and a small hourly wage while training for productive work in society.

7. *Mantua Community Planners*, West Philadelphia, $15,000. This group evolved out of the "Young Great Society" self-help program in the Mantua area. Devoted to helping black people develop and use their own resources, this community-run organization is using our fund's money for the rehabilitation and furnishing of a building for office space, a printing shop, and a community services building.

8. *Welfare Rights Organization*, Philadelphia, $15,000. The purpose of WRO is to organize poor people to fight economic and social oppression. Most of the money from the fund was used to hire an organizer, Mr. Charles Miller. The remaining amount is used for expenses of welfare recipients who come to WRO for training. They learn the state welfare laws, plus organizational techniques, so they can go into their neighborhoods advising poor people of their rights and organizing them into action groups to fight the many injustices which are part of their existence. Since the fund's grant, thirty organizers have been trained and six women have been assigned to VISTA to work among the poor of the city.

9. *Martin Luther King, Jr., School of Social Change*, Chester, Pa., $5,000. Although the school was legally a department of Crozer Seminary, its students were almost all laymen. The school's purpose was to train social change agents for professional roles in society. Our money was used for scholarships. (When Crozer Seminary moved to Rochester, New York, in 1970, the King School was not immediately reorganized.)

10. *Afro-American Industries, Inc.,* Camden, New Jersey, $3,000. This unique industry came into being through the cooperation of the Black People's Unity Movement and the Martin Luther King, Jr., Christian Center, both in Camden, N. J. Manufacturing of colorful Afro garments has met many needs. The business flourished, presently employing twenty persons and selling all that it can produce. Money from our fund purchased eight commercial sewing machines.

11. *Main Line Housing Improvement Corporation,* $15,000. This corporation has spun off from the Main Line Community Association for the purpose of providing decent housing for low-income families within our Main Line area. Specifically, the money from our fund was used to buy four and one-half acres of land in Malvern, Pa. Construction of low-cost homes is planned for 1969-1970.

12. *Ludlow Community Association,* Philadelphia, $3,500. The people of Ludlow have long felt the need of a child day care center. When space becomes available in a new community center being built by Temple Presbyterian Church, King Fund money will be used to furnish the classrooms.

Appendix 7
Statistics

NEW MEMBERS RECEIVED

	Baptized	Letter	Experience	Total	Members Lost Total
1958	4	38	3	45	35
1959	3	71	—	74	35
1960	23	34	—	57	14
1961	20	35	3	58	33
1962	13	49	—	62	35
1963	11	49	—	60	31
1964	15	39	1	55	50
1965	12	57	1	70	28
1966	1	30	3	34	34
1967	12	61	2	75	29
1968	2	86	2	90	33
1969	22	41	—	63	30

STEWARDSHIP GIVING

	Current Expenses	Missions	Total
1960	$43,332	$14,165	$ 57,497
1961	47,731	14,269	62,000
1962	44,890	18,005	62,895
1963	49,696	20,305	70,000
1964	50,057	24,000	74,057
1965	54,225	27,775	82,000
1966	57,725	27,475	85,200
1967	64,031	28,525	92,556
1968	63,900	28,550	92,450
1969	67,400	32,600	100,000

ANALYSIS OF GIVING — 1970

Pledged Amount	Number of families giving this amount
$ 1- 5 a week	45
$ 5-10 a week	50
$10-20 a week	60
$20-50 a week	20
Over $50 a week	2